Hölderlin's Hyperion

A CRITICAL READING

Walter Silz

Hölderlin's Hyperion

A CRITICAL READING

UNIVERSITY OF PENNSYLVANIA PRESS
PHILADELPHIA

University of Pennsylvania Studies
in Germanic Languages and Literatures

Edited by
ANDRÉ VON GRONICKA and OTTO SPRINGER

Copyright © 1969 by the TRUSTEES OF THE UNIVERSITY OF PENNSYLVANIA
Library of Congress Catalog Card Number: 76-97071
SBN: 8122-7609-4
Printed in the United States of America

TO THE BELOVED

Preface

Hyperion oder der Eremit in Griechenland is the only major work that Hölderlin completed, the only original work he saw published in book form during his sane lifetime. It shares countless motifs with his poems, past, contemporaneous, and future; standing in the middle of his all-too-brief production, it gathers up more of his characteristic themes than any other of his writings; and it is the chief monument to the most decisive period of his life. Yet *Hyperion* has been comparatively neglected by Hölderlin scholars in favor of the late hymns, whose obscurities have not always been clarified by the voluminous and frequently conflicting exegeses expended on them.

The following commentary seeks to avoid metaphysics, theory, and construction and to give instead a literary, stylistic criticism of the text of the final edition. "Critical," I realize, is a bad word to many people who maintain that the scholar dealing with a work of recognized greatness must praise and justify it in every detail. My own conviction is that the scholar-critic is not only permitted but obligated to point out the weak as well as the strong features of a work to which he has devoted long and careful study.[1] This view I have tried to exemplify in the following pages.

All references to Hölderlin's works are made to the Grosse Stuttgarter Ausgabe (abbreviated StA) edited by Friedrich Beissner, Stuttgart 1943 ff. As in the third volume (1957) of that edition, the text of *Hyperion* is here cited according to volume (Roman numeral) and page of the first print of the novel (1797 and 1799). Hölderlin's letters are quoted by number and line from the sixth volume (edited by Adolf Beck) of the StA. For the convenience of users of other editions, the sixty letters that constitute *Hyperion* are sometimes referred to by their "unofficial" serial number.

February 1969   WALTER SILZ

---

[1] See my brief discussion, "The Scholar, the Critic, and the Teacher of Literature," in *The German Quarterly*, 37 (1964), 113–119.

Contents

[ix]

Hölderlin's Hyperion

A CRITICAL READING

I. *Convention and Kinship*

A young writer making his debut as a novelist in Germany in the last decade of the eighteenth century could not help being affected by the conventions established by the most successful contemporary types, the *Bildungsroman* and the *Briefroman.* The novel as a genre was in the ascendant and would soon be declared supreme by the Romanticists in theory and practice. The "novel of education," dating from Rousseau and Wieland in the 1760's, and reaching a peak in Goethe's *Lehrjahre* (1795–96) when Hölderlin's work was already under way, told the story of an individual's development from early youth to maturity through experiences of friendship and love, travel and adventure, ideal aspirations and practical and public concerns. Discussions, *Bildungsgespräche,* like the extended one conducted by Hyperion amid the ruins of Athens, a shipwreck, a mysterious stranger, and a secret society such as figure in Alabanda's story, were stock elements in eighteenth-century fiction.

[3]

The hermit figure, aside from being a favorite one in literature, had a personal interest for Hölderlin. In his letters he frequently speaks of his pleasure in solitude and seclusion, and on occasion he plays with the notion of becoming a hermit (StA 6, No. 13, lines 35 ff.; No. 174, 1. 10). A Greek background had been used by Wieland in *Agathon* (1766) and Heinse in *Ardinghello* (1787). It held, of course, a special attraction for Hölderlin, but it is interesting to note that in the same early letter in which he depicts his shining vision of the ancient Greek world he also shrewdly considers its appeal, combined with a love story, to women readers. He thinks too that the hero of his "griechischen Roman," here first mentioned, should prove more entertaining than those of the chivalric romances, "die wort- und abenteuerreichen Ritter." [1] The struggle of the modern Greeks for independence (1770), on which he centered his plot, was still fresh in public memory.

There is, then, some evidence that Hölderlin was practically aware of the contemporary state of the German novel; and he naturally wanted his own work to succeed (a wish betrayed negatively by his Preface). On the other hand, there is little to show that he thought of himself as a bold innovator and of his book as a radical departure in novel form, as Lawrence Ryan maintains.[2] What Hölderlin says in the just-quoted letter to Neuffer about a "*terra incognita* im Reiche der Poësie" (No. 60, lines 61 ff.) cannot be pressed too hard, for Hölderlin is simply agreeing with Neuffer's quite general remark that there is still room for achievement in literature, and Hölderlin adds "especially in the novel" because he is just then eagerly at work

---

[1] To Neuffer, July 1793; StA 6, No. 60, lines 32–39.

[2] Lawrence Ryan, *Hölderlins "Hyperion"*: Exzentrische Bahn und Dichterberuf (Stuttgart, 1965), pp. 1 f.

on one.[3] What "innovation" there is in *Hyperion* is rather
an unconscious one: its unique lyrical-musical character,
which springs from its author's peculiar genius and temper.

Hyperion's closest kinsman in literature is Goethe's
Die Leiden des jungen Werthers. Years ago, Friedrich
Theodor Vischer characterized Hölderlin as "ein grie-
chischer Werther, oder vielmehr ein Werther des Grie-
chentums." [4] This "unglückliche Bonmot," as Friedrich
Beissner calls it (StA 3, 430), was repeated by others and
applied chiefly to *Hyperion.* One can agree with Beissner
in rejecting such a pat formula and yet feel that in rejecting it he divorces the two novels too sharply, underestimates their lyrical component—overemphasized, he finds,
especially in the case of *Hyperion*—and credits the latter
with a superior objectivity which it hardly possesses. *Werther* is the only real predecessor of *Hyperion.* Hölderlin's
novel is of course no "imitation" of Goethe's, yet it is
deeply akin to the earlier work and shows, despite marked
differences, a number of striking similarities and perhaps
unconscious echoes.

Externally, there are obvious likenesses. Both stories
are in the form of letters written by the title hero. The
letters vary in length from a few lines to many pages. As
Werther is divided into two "Bücher," so *Hyperion* is into
two "Bände"—of which the second appeared after an unfortunate delay of over two years, whereas *Werther* burst
upon the public as an effective unit. The second part of
both works is, on the whole, in a minor key, contrasting
with the first part. In both novels the principle of a single

[3] Friedrich Beissner, StA 3, p. 429, narrows Hölderlin's *terra incognita*
to the novel genre; I see no warrant in the text for this.

[4] *Marbacher Schillerbuch* (Stuttgart and Berlin, 1905), p. 285.

letter-writer was evidently aimed at, but not adhered to in the second part: in *Werther* an Editor supervenes to wind up the story in the past tense; in *Hyperion* the hero's correspondence with Diotima is introduced, shifting us, for fifteen of the sixty letters, to the lovers' bygone present; moreover, letters from Alabanda and Notara are quoted or imbedded in Hyperion's. In Hölderlin, the beloved is heard in direct missives of her own; Lotte is seen only through Werther's eyes (and, at the end, the Editor's). The editorial fiction, supported in both novels by an occasional explanatory or defensive footnote, is much more fully developed in *Werther,* necessarily so after the hero dies, as he does not in *Hyperion.*

In the main, Werther writes of immediate, day-to-day experiences, Hyperion writes from retrospect; hence *Werther* impresses us as a real letter or diary record, *Hyperion* more as an elegy, in keeping with the hero's declared "elegischen Karakter" (I, 4), which he shares with his author.

Both novels have been widely regarded as merely "sentimental" tales, and they do speak the emotional language of their time, with much reference to *Herz, Seele,* and *Tränen;* yet both contain substantial thought and timeless wisdom. Werther knows that he is apt "in Verzükkung und Gleichnisse [zu] verfallen" (am 27. Mai) and to overlook practical details; but if the real world sometimes grows "dämmernd" for him, it vanishes entirely at moments for Hyperion, and the high pitch of lyrical utterance in "raptures and similes" is even more sustained in his story.[5]

Werther's frequent procedure in letter writing, which he admits is not "historisch" (am 17. Mai, end), is well illus-

---

[5] The word and concept "dämmern" is a characteristic favorite in both works.

trated by the famous letter "am 16. Junius": he starts in the middle in a state of emotional excitement and only after some time comes around to the beginning and an orderly report. Hyperion's procedure is often similar: his fourth letter, for instance, opens with an emotional recall, and it is some time before its human subject, Adamas, is even mentioned; then comes a lengthy apostrophe to him, before the correspondent is told who he was or what importance he had for Hyperion; only after thirty-odd lines does the writer begin on an approximately "historical" account (I, 18, 14 ff.). He too half apologizes: "ich hätte Lust, so pünktlich dir, wie Nestor, zu erzählen" (I, 22, 14).

The introduction of the heroine is somewhat in this manner in both works: she is not brought in at the start, but after a rich prelude of *Naturbegeisterung*. Both writers begin far afield, expressing their feeling in rhapsodic language and only then naming its cause. Hyperion refers to his beloved as "das Göttliche," "die Schönheit," "der Frieden," and only after a dozen pages identifies her as Diotima (I, 94, 9). Even after that, when he comes to narrate the sequence of events, he is not nearly so concrete as Werther. The conception of love, "romantic" and spiritualized in both stories, reaches a higher degree of immateriality in Hölderlin's. There is little of physical love in *Werther,* and almost none in *Hyperion.*

However different the plots of the two novels are, the possibility of a *Werther*-like complication is recognized by Alabanda as a reason for his final departure. When he says "Glaube mir, es ist gewagt, um Liebende zu leben, und ein thatlos Herz, wie meines nun ist, hält es schwerlich aus" (II, 81), he is approximately summing up Werther's situation; and Alabanda's fear that he might in the end murder Diotima and kill himself (II, 88)—a bizarre and uncharacteristic notion—might be a far echo from Werther, who is haunted by the idea of killing Albert, Lotte, and himself ("den ein und zwanzigsten Dezember," says the *Herausgeber.*) In withdrawing from the threatening triangle to a sure death, Alabanda is making good Werther's words "eins von uns dreien muß hinweg, und das will ich sein" (*ibid.*).

The first glimpse of Lotte that so entranced Werther: Lotte in her dual role of sister/mother with a brood of young children crowding around her—"das reizendste Schauspiel . . . , das ich je gesehen habe" (am 16. Junius)—may conceivably have inspired similar pictures of motherly and sisterly love in *Hyperion:* "Wie, wenn die Mutter schmeichelnd frägt, wo um sie her ihr Liebstes sey, und alle Kinder in den Schoos ihr stürzen . . ." (I, 87/88); or "Wie eine Schwester, wenn aus jeder Eke ein Geliebtes ihr entgegenkömmt, und jedes gerne zuerst gegrüßt seyn möchte . . ." (I, 100).

One major area of sensibility which the two novels share is a fervent *Naturgefühl,* a passionate, ecstatic experience of loving oneness with Nature, "der Geliebten." An intense delight in the beauty of the phenomenal world is deepened by a pantheistic belief in its divinity, a conviction of the presence of God or gods in all creation—an attitude that interfuses aesthetic, religious, and erotic emotions. Hyperion's posture in the beginning, when he lies amid flowers and grasses at Nature's bosom and gazes longingly up at the sky (I, 15), reminds us of a picture with similar features in an early letter of Werther's (am 10. Mai). Both men feel the desire to lose themselves in Nature. Werther finally yields up his life to this pull toward the infinite, universal being; Hyperion the hermit forsakes the world of men to become "Priester der göttlichen Natur." For both, the end is escape from the bonds of society.

[8]

The background of Nature, the progression of the seasons, is used in both works, more fully and with more conscious art in *Werther,* to give resonance and depth to human actions and moods. There is, for example, in the fourth letter a sustained passage recalling the boy Hyperion's happy spring wanderings with his teacher Adamas ("Aber dreifach fühlt' ich . . ."), a sentence of twenty-odd lines that climbs a long slope of *wenn*-clauses, catches its breath in a dash, and descends in a shorter conclusion (I, 21,10–22,13); this has a close counterpart in the rhapsodic sentence beginning "Wenn das liebe Tal um mich dampft . . ." in Werther's second letter (am 10. Mai).

There is the brief but brilliant "Herbstbild" that opens the second volume and sets its minor key: afterglow of a more primal fire, wistful remembrance of joys past, suggestion of farewells to come (II, 3). Another terse autumn picture, conveying the "großer, stiller, zärtlicher Geist dieser Jahrszeit," seconds the mood of the convalescent hero after the battle (II, 63, 9–14). Sometimes, on the other hand, the Nature scene subtly contradicts the human mood. Thus, on a later day, Hyperion is sitting, carefree, with Alabanda, enjoying the warm sunlight; but the fallen leaves scudding in the wind, the felled tree that breaks the stillness of the landscape, the murmur of a transient brook (II, 79, 7–11) all are ominous of change and tragedy soon to erupt.

Shifts from a positive to a negative value in events, persons, and also natural settings are more systematically employed as a structural principle in *Werther,* but *Hyperion* is not without them. Thus, in a dejected mood, Hyperion feels the approach of autumn storms, and Nature, erstwhile so ebullient and gay, now faces him morose and silent, like himself (I, 39). The heroes of both stories conceive themselves as Nature's lovers: Hyperion stands before

[9]

her, "der Geliebte vor der Geliebten" (I, 10). But she can also fold her arms and show him an alien face: "und ich stehe, wie ein Fremdling, vor ihr, und verstehe sie nicht" (I, 11). Werther, on his last day, speaks to Nature as "dein Geliebter"; but she too, once so radiant and alive, can present the aspect of "ein lackiertes Bildchen" without depth or meaning (am 3. November). In a hopeful, jubilant mood Hyperion pitches his tent on the Eurotas and throws a tribute of flowers into its sparkling waves (II, 42).[6] After the military debacle, this natural feature, like those in the second part of *Werther,* reappears with negative significance: "Am Eurotas hat mein Leben sich müde geweint, ach! am Eurotas, der in rettungsloser Schmach an Lacedämons Schutt vorüberklagt, mit allen seinen Wellen" (II, 49).

Certain other natural features are emphasized in both novels. Trees are regarded with special interest and affection; they are closely related to persons and all but personified; they are referred to with a loving possessive as "mein Wald," "meine Bäume." What a role, happy and unhappy, the *Nußbäume* of the parsonage play in Werther's experience! "O meine alten freundlichen Bäume!" Diotima cries out, as to close friends, witnesses now to her new happiness (I, 128) and later to her withering (II, 97). Hyperion associates with her trees as with personal friends: "Ich war ja indessen so oft mit diesen Bäumen umgegangen" (I, 127). To come "von Diotima's Bäumen" is equivalent to coming "von ihr" (I, 114, 1 f.).

In *Werther,* trees are connected at once with the recurring motif of the well, which figures also in *Hyperion.* The picture of Werther sitting by his "lieber Brunnen"

[6] The motif is anticipated in Hyperion's youth, when he cast an offering of flowers into the Meles in honor of Homer (I, 32).

(am 6. Julius) and imagining beneficent spirits hovering around it (am 12. Mai) may have suggested the scene in Hyperion's last letter in which, sitting by a solitary German *Brunnen,* he experiences Diotima's spiritual return.

Closely related to the realm of Nature, equally endowed with divinity, is the world of the child. Both authors give it superlative praise; both use it not only as a poetic motif but as an ethical standard to measure the adult world. The third letter, in which Hyperion begins the story of his life, opens with a eulogy of childhood, its innocence, its wholeness, its beauty in contrast to the impoverished "adjusted" elders who seek to degrade the child and distort it into their own image (I, 13 f.). Werther is likewise convinced of the ill effect of adults on children and the vicious circle of education: "sie bilden ihre Kinder nach sich und . . . [so wird es nie besser]" (am 29. Junius). Aside from a rare specific observation of child behavior, however (I, 89, 1 ff.), Hölderlin's view of childhood is highly idealized and general, whereas Goethe's is far more realistic and varied.

The pretensions of "cultivated" society arouse Hyperion's scorn as they do Werther's. He reports Adamas's disappointment in "der sogenannten kultivierten Welt" (I, 19), and he himself, when he goes about "unter diesen Gebildeten," is reminded of varieties of animals (I, 35). Werther exclaims indignantly "Wir Gebildeten—zu Nichts Verbildeten" (am 4. September), and habitually exalts the primitive above degenerate society.[7] In particular, the bourgeois counsel of useful industry, *Aktivität* and *Handeln* as virtues in themselves, is spurned by both heroes (Hyperion's first letter, Werther's of "20. Julius"). The dis-

[7] In both authors the criticism of society, as well as the enthusiasm for Nature and childhood, show the influence of Rousseau.

traught query "aber was soll mir das?" [*mir* stressed] in this opening letter, seemingly an echo of that at the end of Werther's letter of "30. November," is more than a mere phrase for both men: it sums up their tragic awareness of being misfits in the social world.[8]

Yet they both to some extent "go along with" social pretense. Werther writes of its empty "Schwall," but adds "Ich spiele mit, vielmehr ich werde gespielt wie eine Marionette, und fasse manchmal meinen Nachbar an der hölzernen Hand" (am 20. Januar). In like vein Hyperion views the "Possenspiel" and joins it: "Oft ließ ich sogar mir gefallen, mitzumachen, und wenn ich noch so seelenlos, so ohne eignen Trieb dabei war, das merkte keiner" (I, 70).

Hyperion has, like Werther, an extremely active sense of the past; he too is a "Wiederkäuer des Vergangenen." In his very first letter, Werther promises to reform in this respect. He agrees that our troubles would be lessened if human nature did not prefer a painful past to an insipid present: "die Erinnerungen des vergangenen Übels zurückzurufen, eher, als eine gleichgültige Gegenwart zu ertragen." In a similar reflection Hyperion asks himself why he chooses to revive past sufferings by writing his story, and he answers: all these experiences are part of our life, and to suppress them for the sake of peace of mind would impoverish our present existence (II, 20). It is characteristic of the two men that they undertake what they both call a *Wallfahrt* in quest of an irrecoverable past glory: Werther to his childhood home, Hyperion to the ruins of Athens.[9]

Disillusioned in his first encounter with the world and with friendship, Hyperion longs to withdraw to his native

---

[8] There is what seems a more extended echo of Werther's words in Hölderlin's poem *Abendphantasie:* see my edition of *German Romantic Lyrics* (Cambridge, 1934), p. 254.

[9] *Werther,* am 9. Mai; *Hyperion,* I, 137, 11.

island and home garden. He recognizes this expanding-contracting rhythm as basic in the life process: "Bestehet ja das Leben der Welt im Wechsel des Entfaltens und Verschließens, in Ausflug und in Rükkehr zu sich selbst, warum nicht auch das Herz des Menschen?" (I, 65). So Werther in an early letter philosophizes "über die Begier im Menschen, sich auszubreiten, neue Entdeckungen zu machen, herumzuschweifen; und dann wieder über den innern Trieb, sich der Einschränkung willig zu ergeben. . . . So sehnt sich der unruhigste Vagabund zuletzt wieder nach seinem Vaterlande" (am 21. Junius). For Goethe, as we know, such recognitions led to a law of polarity manifested in phenomena like the diastole and systole of the heart. Hyperion comes eventually to accept life's two-phasedness and expresses it in the striking final figure of the veins parting and reuniting in the heart.

After the breakup of his friendship with Alabanda, a suicide mood comes over Hyperion for a moment as he stands at the brink of the ocean: "ach! da hinunter strebte mein Herz, da hinunter, und meine Arme flogen der freien Fluth entgegen" (I, 64). So Werther had stood at the brink of the winter flood: "Ach mit offenen Armen stand ich gegen den Abgrund und atmete hinab! hinab!" (am 12. Dezember). Both men regard suicide as the premature termination of an ordained course that calls for special justification: Werther, in an earlier letter, thinks of it, in more Christian terms, as a cutting short of life's pilgrimage and a return, unbidden and *unvermutet,* to a forgiving Father (am 30. November); Hyperion, mindful of Empedokles, conceives the act in more pagan terms as flinging oneself, *ungerufen,* at the heart of Nature (II, 110).[10]

[10] The suicide note, struck early in *Werther:* "das süße Gefühl der Freiheit, und daß er diesen Kerker verlassen kann, wann er [der Mensch] will" (am 22. Mai), echoes still in a later Hölderlin poem: "Und verstehe

At one point in his story, Hyperion remarks that Bellarmin should notice in his handwriting that he is growing quieter: "ich meine, du solltest sogar meinen Briefen es ansehn, wie meine Seele täglich stiller wird und stiller" (II, 21). So Werther, reporting the fate of the "Bauerbursch," expected Wilhelm to notice the unusual calm in his hand: "Ich bin heute still, indem ich das hinschreibe; du siehst an meiner Hand, daß ich nicht so strudele und sudele wie sonst." [11]

In an earlier version of the novel, *Hyperions Jugend*, Diotima asks Hyperion to read aloud passages he has copied from a rare book—as Lotte had suggested that Werther read from his Ossian translation. In her absence, Hyperion had tuned her harp, as Werther did Lotte's piano (StA 3, p. 231). The young hero imagines himself standing, greatly agitated, before the beloved: "ich . . . faßte ihre Hände zum erstenmale, und drükte sie so mit Zittern an meine Stirne" (StA 3, p. 225). Just so Werther, at the end of the reading of Ossian, had thrown himself down before Lotte, "faßte ihre Hände, drückte sie in seine Augen, wider seine Stirn."

The radiant picture of sunrise over rain-drenched woods, "der tröpfelnde Wald," after the thunderstorm in *Werther* (am 19. Junius) has its counterpart in the "tröpfelnden Walde" after refreshing rain in *Hyperion* (I, 15). In somberer mood, Werther's compassionate vision of "der

---

die Freiheit, / Aufzubrechen, wohin er [der Mensch] will" (*Lebenslauf*, longer version). In letter as in poem, the thought is put in emphatic final position.

[11] "Am 4. September." The situation, mood (humility induced by another's suffering), and wording are not unlike those in a later letter of Hyperion's: "jezt . . . , indem ich diß erzähle . . . ich bin ruhig," etc. (II, 106).

unaufhaltsam hinabstürzenden Kreatur" (am 15. November) may have provided the germ of the final image of Hyperion's "Schiksaalslied." Both young authors have a tragic sense for helpless, afflicted humanity, and the figure of the madman vainly seeking flowers out of season (am 30. November) seems a weird anticipation of the later Hölderlin himself and his plaint in *Hälfte des Lebens*.

The compositional art of striking letter endings is exemplified in both these epistolary novels. Perhaps the supreme example among many in *Hyperion* is that which in the thirty-sixth letter terminates a scene of farewell in a spirit of infinity and all but superhuman *Vergeistigung*. The starry sky is decreed to be the lovers' meeting-ground henceforth, when words no longer avail. "Das sei er!" says Diotima, "mit einem langsamen niegehörten Tone—es war ihr lezter. Im Dämmerlichte entschwand mir ihr Bild und ich weiß nicht, ob sie es wirklich war, da ich zum leztenmale mich umwandt' und die erlöschende Gestalt noch einen Augenblik vor meinem Auge zükte und dann in die Nacht verschied" (II, 19/20). One is reminded of the brilliant "fade-out" at the end of the first book of *Werther*, which likewise terminates a scene of farewell. But how much more concrete is Goethe's: a definite locale, a familiar garden, soft moonlight. Hölderlin has no setting, hardly persons, but two souls immediate to the stars of cosmic space, and words that anticipate the finality of death; these lovers never meet again. The materiality of life is here almost unbearably attenuated. Diotima's person has been rarified, etherialized: "zart, wie der Aether, umwand mich Diotima" (II, 19). The light grows dim, eyesight fails, and at the last Hyperion is not even sure that it is she whose "expiring" form quivers for an instant before him to "die into the night." Goethe's scene, for all its high-strung emotion, is still dramatic, plastic, and earthly; Hölderlin's is a sublime, metaphysical lyric.

Hölderlin's personal contacts with Goethe were grotesque fiascos, and Goethe's estimate of the younger poet ranks among his major misjudgments. Nor does Hölderlin, on his part, appear to have been much affected by Goethe's works. With *Werther,* however, he must have felt a deep affinity to which his creative mind responded.

II. *A Novel in Letters*

One device of eighteenth-century fiction that did not work wholly to the advantage of *Hyperion* was the letter form— as Hölderlin chose to employ it. In *Werther,* Goethe had improved on his predecessors in the epistolary novel by reducing the medley of voices virtually to one. This greatly furthered artistic unity and, thanks to Werther's lively human sympathy and vivid power of expression, his canvas does not lack variety of portraiture. Hölderlin to some extent returned to the older form of multiple correspondents (besides the hero's, letters by Diotima, Notara, and Alabanda are included); but *Hyperion* is still in the main a monologue and in the main one in the past tense.

Hölderlin had not Goethe's power of character drawing which by indirection could make even Wilhelm a personality; Bellarmin is completely colorless and unresponsive, a nonentity who adds nothing to the novel or its letter fiction. Aside from the statement (at the beginning of the third letter) that he has asked Hyperion for his story, there is no indication that Bellarmin ever writes to him. Near the end, Bellarmin is said to have inquired what his friend's state of mind is after he has related his most tragic experience: "und du fragst, mein Bellarmin! wie jezt mir ist, indem ich diß erzähle?" (II, 106, 11 f.). But this must be a question Hyperion puts to himself; no correspondent could possibly have timed it so well. It has a counterpart in an earlier query: "Frägst du, wie mir gewesen sey um diese Zeit?" (I, 113, 18), which is equally "reflexive." What Hyperion says at the end of the novel is not "Write again," but only "More anon" (from me). Bellarmin is little more than a form of address. No dialogue is developed in this one-sided correspondence.

There is something self-contradictory about letters as here used, retrospectively. Letters are by nature a vehicle of direct, immediate communication; here, they are used like records of the past, memoirs accompanied by commentary in the present. Werther's letters keep us abreast of a developing situation and action; they are enlivening and suspenseful. But to resort to letters to recount earlier experiences in instalments is artificial and can be confusing. There is no inherent reason for cutting off a *past* story into letters, instead of telling it as a continuous narrative in the first person.

Hyperion differs fundamentally from *Werther* in having an omniscient hero, not merely an omniscient author. These letters are written (in some cases copied and hence no longer "live") at a remove by a reminiscent hero who knows the outcome and has survived it, not by a hero passionately, mortally involved in unfolding events. The resultant loss in immediacy and tension is very great, and only a writer of non-dramatic, lyrical-elegiac temper would have adopted such a distancing procedure. Wilhelm Michel, in his excellent biography,[1] argues that Hölderlin chose it, instead of straightforward "epische Erzählung," because he needed "das lebendige Gegenüber"—but does the lifeless Bellarmin answer this description, and is anything approaching "die Situation eines gegenwärtigen Gespräches" created?

The letters-in-retrospect device creates a difficulty throughout. The entire account thereby becomes *post factum,* and the narrating hero cannot be kept entirely separated from the experiencing one. It is seldom demonstrable which ideas he had at the time reported and which he has evolved since. The shift in time levels, now present (where a real exchange is inserted), now recollected, not only tends to confuse the reader but disturbs the characterization of the hero. In *Werther* we start with a clean slate: we know Werther's state of mind "as of" the beginning and we follow his course as experienced—with the additional help of datelines. Hyperion's course is not equally clear. Hölderlin presents him in part as a man at the beginning, in part as a man at the end, of a series of experiences, and gives us glimpses at other points; but the upshot, the extent to which the resolution, the "Auflösung der Dissonanzen" announced in the Preface, is accomplished, remains uncertain.

In *Hyperion,* unlike *Werther,* the end is not the end. Lawrence Ryan,[2] indeed, calls attention to the fact that the close of the novel sets forth views which the hero has renounced in favor of more mature and valid insights stated a number of pages earlier, in the narrator's present, while his closing statement belongs to his abandoned past. But

[1] Wilhelm Michel, *Das Leben Friedrich Hölderlins* (Darmstadt, 1963), pp. 133 f.

[2] L. Ryan, *Hölderlins "Hyperion,"* p. 226.

can a novel so arranged be credited with "eine Geschlossen-
heit des Aufbaus, die in der Romankunst der klassisch-
romantischen deutschen Literatur wohl ihresgleichen
sucht" (*ibid.*)? And Mr. Ryan is by no means alone in this
high praise of the structure of *Hyperion* as a novel.[3] To me
it seems that praise must rest on other grounds.

In the first Book of the second volume, a sequence of
fifteen letters is inserted, constituting the lovers' correspondence during the military campaign, all laboriously
copied out now for Bellarmin (II, 59, 2 f.). For this interval, then, we leave the prevailing tense of historical retrospect and enter a pseudo-present. It is not clear what the
author gains compositionally by this displacement of time
strata. The only real reason Hyperion offers is that he
could not tell his friend how much he (Hyperion) was
loved; only Diotima can say that (II, 21). This, however,
is not convincing in view of his success heretofore in telling
just that in his own words and in extensive quotation
from hers!

Over long stretches of *Hyperion*, the letters are simply
sections of an *Ich-Erzählung* and do not have the character
of a true correspondence. For instance, the one that follows the enclave just mentioned and opens the second
Book of the second volume has a short introductory paragraph addressed to Bellarmin and at the end an oblique

---

[3] See, for example, H.-W. Bertallot, *Hölderlin-Nietzsche* (Berlin, 1933),
p. 71: "eine im höchsten Grade organische, geschlossene Kompositionsform"
(see also pp. 34, 38); H. H. Borcherdt, *Der Roman der Goethezeit* (Urach-
Stuttgart, 1949), p. 360: "in unerhörter Klarheit der Gliederung wird hier
der Bildungsweg Hyperions umrissen und jede einzelne Stufe gesondert
entwickelt"; Beissner, StA 3, pp. 430 f.: "meisterliche Gesamtkomposition,
. . . hohe und sichere Kunst des Erzählers . . . klar ausgewogener Kunst-
gestalt . . . schönem Maß und Verhältnis der Teile im Gesamtaufbau" (see
also p. 489).

reference to him, but no real congé. The next three letters have no word for him whatever. The last of them is actually made up of a letter of Diotima's and one of Hyperion's, in effect a continuation of their *Briefwechsel* just mentioned. The third letter from the end is inordinately long; it incorporates a lyric poem, a letter from Diotima extending over five instalments, plus a letter from Notara and Hyperion's reply to it. All these inserts and present-within-past letters, moreover, are found in the second volume; the first had consisted of thirty "straight" missives from Hyperion to Bellarmin; so it appears that Hölderlin made his letter-machinery more cumbersome as he proceeded.

We must assume, though it is nowhere stated (there is no editorial motivation, as in *Werther*), that the ultimate custodian, Bellarmin, a German, has published these letters written by Greeks. We must assume, furthermore, that Hyperion either had made copies of his correspondence with Diotima and Notara, or got his originals back from them (though he tells us he never returned to Kalaurea). Either procedure must seem prosaic and chilling. The same would hold for Hyperion's long last letter to Notara (II, 107–112), written in Sicily on his way to Germany.

We must make the sober assumption, too, that the estranged friends have kept each other duly informed of their mailing addresses, else how would Hyperion have known where in Smyrna to direct his letters (I, 76), and how could Alabanda have known that Hyperion had thereafter gone to stay in Kalaurea, an unforeseeable move? With the prospect of war, nevertheless, the relationship resumes: "Es war ein Brief von Alabanda gekommen" (his only one, II, 5 f.)—as though there had been no rupture but a steady correspondence.

For the novel plot in Greece, the letter business seems

artificial, where distances are so short, and it becomes contrived as *Boten* and *Diener* come and go and develop-
ments depend on their arrival too early or too late. Thus,
just as Hyperion has ended his *Schiksaalslied,* with unlikely timing a boat comes in, bringing his servant, who
had been sent with a crucial letter and who now delivers
Diotima's last reply. It is characteristic of Hölderlin's indifference to dramatic possibilities that this man, and the
scene he must have witnessed in Kalaurea, are not in the
least degree visualized. Only from the beginning of Diotima's letter do we even learn that it was not complete, and
she already dead, before the man arrived. For she had lived
an agonizing week in the conviction that her lover had met
the death he sought in battle. His fatal letter had come all
too fast, his revocation too slowly. In the interval her fate
was sealed. The epistolary machinery is dubious enough
when it involves lost letters: two of Diotima's to Hyperion
(II, 67) and apparently three of his to Alabanda (I, 76) fail
to arrive. But when heartbreak and death ensue, our minds
protest: faulty mail service should not be a factor in tragedy.

It seems implausible that the hero's account of what
happened is just as detailed in his present letters to Bellarmin (which are based on memory) as in those written at
that past time and now copied for his friend. It is unlikely
that Hyperion could recall verbatim conversations of years
ago. The emotional turmoil in some passages strikes us as
improbable in a retrospecting writer long after the event.
Here, again, past and present merge confusingly. The long
Athens lecture is incredible in its remembered detail and
pedantic in a letter to a friend. One wonders, too, why
Hyperion did not tell his story to Bellarmin when they
were together in Germany, instead of waiting until he had

returned to Greece and sending it in letters. And why should a hermit, who has turned his back on the world of men, be wanting to tell them of his life? An author desirous of a public inevitably peeps through the conventional costume.

It is Mr. Ryan's thesis (*op. cit.*, e.g. pp. 4, 105) that Hyperion develops and matures during and through the act of writing these letters. But can one ascribe so great an effect to the mere mental hygiene of communication? The determinative events that Hyperion relates lie concluded behind him; no important new experiences occur during the writing. Is it credible that he has not come to terms with his past until now, that insight should wait upon this epistolary activity? Would this not argue a thoughtless man who has seen no meaning in his life and sees it only now, in complying with another's request for his autobiography? In sum, is it possible to justify the letter form, as here employed, on grounds of plot, characterization, and structure? I do not believe it is.

Nevertheless, the device of letters-in-retrospect produces some memorable specimens of prose poetry.[4] For one thing, Hölderlin seems to have devoted conscious art to his letter openings and letter closings to give them a special revelatory force or sententious weight. They may be lapidary summaries or vivid evocations or generalized *Sentenzen;* they may state and recapitulate the theme of a letter or "frame" its substance. Thus the opening of the very first letter: "Der liebe Vaterlandsboden giebt mir wieder

---

[4] In this connection it seems worth noting that Hyperion's letters in the direct exchange (2. Band, 1. Buch) are not particularly poetic; only in the last two of them, after he considers his bond with Diotima broken and he looks back on it (II, 49–56), does he recover his high tone—another evidence of Hölderlin's lyric-elegiac genius.

Freude und Laid," brief though it is, expresses not only the
hero's love of his native land, to which he has returned
after a long absence, but his ambivalent attitude toward it.
In a deeper sense, it foreshadows at the outset an acceptance of life's duality that Diotima affirms in her last spoken
words: "Beides [Leiden und Freudigkeit] ist, . . . und
beides ist gut" (II, 19), but which Hyperion even now
(*after* all the experiences soon to be related!) has not firmly
made his own. The close of the letter in turn anticipates
the close of the novel with its turning away from Man to
Nature: "Ja, vergiß nur, daß es Menschen giebt, darbendes,
angefochtenes, tausendfach geärgertes Herz! und kehre
wieder dahin, wo du ausgiengst, in die Arme der Natur,
der wandellosen, stillen und schönen." Stylistically, this is
Hölderlinian in its antithesis and balance and its triadic
pattern: two trios of adjectives, one placed before the
noun, the other chiastically after. The last three words
form the Adonic measure ($'x x 'x$) that is Hölderlin's
favorite closing cadence.

The keynote of the fifth letter, which tells of the writer's happy youth, is sounded in the opening sentence:
"Wohin könnt' ich mir entfliehen, hätt' ich nicht die
lieben Tage meiner Jugend?" (I, 27). In another case, the
opening announces suspensefully a rare mood for the relation of a rare experience: "Mir ist lange nicht gewesen, wie
jezt" (I, 85). The ending of this letter, with its imagery of
fire and liberation, its Herakles note, and its beautiful final
rhythm "im Triumphe zurük in die Hallen der Sonne"
(I, 92 f.) is one of the most sublime in the series.[5]

[5] The fire imagery, a favorite with Hölderlin, anticipates Nietzsche.
The notion of "Feuer, das . . . im Kiesel schläft" is probably derived from
Lessing's *Laokoon*, 1. Abschnitt: "Bei ihm [dem Griechen] war der Herois-
mus wie die verborgenen Funken im Kiesel, die ruhig schlafen, solange
keine äußere Gewalt sie wecket," etc. The reference to the Greeks would
especially have drawn Hölderlin's attention.

The long thirtieth letter, which forms the climax and conclusion of the first volume, preludes with solemn words that prepare us for momentous events: "Es giebt große Stunden im Leben. Wir schauen an ihnen hinauf, wie an den kolossalischen Gestalten der Zukunft und des Altertums, wir kämpfen einen herrlichen Kampf mit ihnen, und bestehn wir vor ihnen, so werden sie, wie Schwestern, und verlassen uns nicht" (I, 136). The conviction of the quality of life, the obligation of measuring up to its supreme hours, the classical imagery, the closing cadence with its choriamb ($'x x'$) that is another favorite termination— all are deeply Hölderlinian.

Often, the opening is a sententious generalization: "Es kann nichts wachsen, und nichts so tief vergehen, wie der Mensch" (I, 74). This may be doubled, with a parallelism and inversion that Hölderlin is fond of:

> Es giebt ein Vergessen alles Daseyns, ein Verstummen unsers Wesens, wo uns ist, als hätten wir alles gefunden.
> Es giebt ein Verstummen, ein Vergessen alles Daseyns, wo uns ist, als hätten wir alles verloren (I, 72 f.)

Akin to this in contrast and paradox is an opening like "Frägst du, wie mir gewesen sey um diese Zeit? Wie einem, der alles verloren hat, um alles zu gewinnen" (I, 113). The influence of the Bible in such passages is unmistakable.

The twenty-third letter commences with a long, suspended paragraph almost in one breath:

> Es ist umsonst, ich kann's mir nicht verbergen. Wohin ich auch entfliehe mit meinen Gedanken, in die Himmel hinauf und in den Abgrund, zum Anfang und an's Ende der Zeiten, selbst wenn ich ihm, der meine lezte Zuflucht war, der sonst noch jede Sorge in mir verzehrte, der alle Lust und allen Schmerz des Lebens sonst mit der Feuer-

flamme, worinn er sich offenbarte, in mir versengte, selbst
wenn ich ihm mich in die Arme werfe, dem herrlichen
geheimen Geiste der Welt, in seine Tiefe mich tauche, wie
in den bodenlosen Ocean hinab, auch da, auch da finden
die süßen Schreken mich aus, die süßen verwirrenden töd-
tenden Schreken, daß Diotima's Grab mir nah ist.
Hörst du? hörst du? Diotima's Grab! (I, 106)

In all its emotional tumult, this is a beautifully structured
utterance, with its repetitions and antitheses, its suspense
rising from beginning to end and enclosing within itself
another suspense (the identity of the "ihm" of the fourth
line), its reiterated climax, "Diotima's Grab!"

The letter endings, even more impressive than the
beginnings, are often distinguished by a vivid, arresting
image. Thus the second letter ends, in a triadic pattern and
Biblical diction characteristic of Hölderlin, "O ein Gott ist
der Mensch, wenn er träumt, ein Bettler, wenn er nach-
denkt, und wenn die Begeisterung hin ist, steht er da, wie
ein misrathener Sohn, den der Vater aus dem Hause stieß,
und betrachtet die ärmlichen Pfennige, die ihm das Mit-
leid auf den Weg gab" (I, 12). The third letter has a sensuous, drastic final picture for Hyperion's uncertainty about
God: "es ist, als fühlt' ich ihn, den Geist der Welt, wie eines
Freundes warme Hand, aber ich erwache und meine, ich
habe meine eignen Finger gehalten" (I, 16). Again, longing for the liberation of death, he sees himself as a prisoner
chained in life's dungeon: "ich schmachte an der Kette
und hasche mit bitterer Freude die kümmerliche Schaale,
die meinem Durste gereicht wird" (I, 30).[6] The next letter, on the other hand, ends with an etherial premonition

---

[6] In this case the terminal image is set off as a new paragraph and
hence can easily be mistaken as relating to the letter-writer's present time;
but it is still dependent on "sprach ich" (I, 30, 11).

of the beloved and the Hölderlinian motif of the lily: "Wie in schweigender Luft sich eine Lilie wiegt, so regte sich in seinem Elemente, in den entzükenden Träumen von ihr, mein Wesen" (I, 38).

Two letters expressing disillusionment with the contemporary world point up their conclusions with striking figures from Nature on a larger and smaller scale: men, says the eighth letter, have lost their faith in greatness and must perish "wenn dieser Glaube nicht wiederkehrt, wie ein Komet aus fremden Himmeln"; resigned indifference, in the ninth letter, lets the world go by: "Wie ein Strom an dürren Ufern, wo kein Weidenblatt im Wasser sich spiegelt, lief unverschönert vorüber an mir die Welt" (I, 72, 74).

Summarizing generalizations often stand at the end: "Was ist alles, was in Jahrtausenden die Menschen thaten und dachten, gegen Einen Augenblick der Liebe? Es ist aber auch das Gelungenste, Göttlichschönste in der Natur! dahin führen alle Stuffen auf der Schwelle des Lebens. Daher kommen wir, dahin gehen wir" (I, 98; see also the two following letters). A sudden access of despair suggests a vision of a savagery rare in Hölderlin: "Das Steuer ist in die Wooge gefallen und das Schiff wird, wie an den Füßen ein Kind, ergriffen und an die Felsen geschleudert" (I, 136).[7] But the next letter concludes the first volume in confident tones of solemn prophecy: "Es wird nur Eine Schönheit seyn; und Menschheit und Natur wird sich vereinen in Eine allumfassende Gottheit" (I, 160). The recognition of transiency and inescapable tragedy culminates in pathos like that of Schiller's *Nänie*: "wer darf sagen, er stehe vest, wenn auch das Schöne seinem Schiksaal so entgegenreift,

---

[7] One is reminded of a similar atrocity in Kleist's *Erdbeben in Chili*. Perhaps both go back to a common source in Greek literature!

wenn auch das Göttliche sich demüthigen muß, und die Sterblichkeit mit allem Sterblichen theilen!" (II, 5). A late letter ends a beautiful, sustained valedictory with the sad recognition "es kann der Mensch nichts ändern und das Licht des Lebens kommt und scheidet, wie es will" (II, 112).

Sometimes there is a subtle duplicity of implication in the letter endings. Thus the opulent *Nachtbild* in which Alabanda exults after his reunion with Hyperion: "Himmel der Nacht, . . . wie eine Rebenlaube überwölbest du mich, und deine Sterne hängen, wie Trauben, herunter" (II, 29/30), for all its sensuous beauty, represents an illusion, for the youth he has apostrophized is forever lost, and the stars, so seemingly close, belong to another world. There is a similar ambiguity in the close of a later letter: Hyperion is comforting himself with the hope that a specially speeded message to Diotima will have set everything right. But the trees shudder in the evening wind, and the stars, those solemn symbols of constancy which the lovers had invoked at their final parting, shine forth from the dark, bespeaking eternity: "Der Bäume Gipfel schauerten leise; wie Blumen aus der dunklen Erde, sproßten Sterne aus dem Schoose der Nacht und des Himmels Frühling glänzt' in heiliger Freude mich an" (II, 66).[8]

Some of these letters are of eminently artistic structure, for example the twenty-fifth letter (I, 109 f.), to which Friedrich Beissner has called attention in his editorial notes (StA 3, 459). It shows Hölderlin's wonted triadic arrangement and a marked symmetry and inversion. Two equally long paragraphs, one beginning "Wenn ich . . . ," the other "Wenn sie . . . ," both couched in the third person,

---

[8] Hyperion's hope is speedily dashed by Diotima's fateful letter (II, 67), which is delivered in the evening—realistically regarded, an unlikely hour.

are followed by a shorter third paragraph which advances to second-person address and shifts from "wenn" to "da." The letter opens with a declarative "Eh' es eines von uns beeden wußte, gehörten wir uns an," and after a steady intensification of feeling, supported by repeated "wenn"s, culminates in an interrogative "Gehörten wir da nicht längst uns an?"—so that with charming paradox, as Beissner points out, the theme of the letter is formulated as an affirmative statement at the beginning and the proven result, the Q E D, as a question at the end. After three paragraphs which are really long subordinate clauses, each ending suspended in a dash, this last sentence, the principal clause, releases a syntactical and emotional tension that has extended through the entire letter.

The following number has a somewhat similar if less elaborated structure: three or four lines of mood and meditation in the present tense at beginning and end, forming a slender "frame" around a vividly remembered incident from the past. A little dramatic scene, more effective than the much longer one at Athens, epitomizes Hyperion's Hellenism, his elegiac-prophetic-pedagogical character, his *Kulturphilosophie,* his idea of *Wiederkehr.* Diotima too reveals herself through action and speech in her bright, warm, loyal, enthusiastic nature. The climax of the letter is her proud epitaph for her beloved: she imagines a future, nobler race saying at his tomb "er wäre, wie unser einer, wär' er jezt da."

III. *End and Beginning*

An unfortunate result of the letter form, as already indicated, is to put the final outcome in an uncertain light.
One naturally looks to the end of a novel as speaking its
last word, and we feel that the author so intended it in this
case; but his arrangement has blurred the intention. The
final letter tells us that the hero has abandoned human society ("ich hab ihn ausgeträumt, von Menschendingen den
Traum") and dedicated himself to Nature as the only living permanence ("und sage, nur du lebst"). He becomes a
hermit; for that fact, which is sometimes overlooked, we
have the clear testimony of the subtitle. Serene and secure,
he sees all things gathered up in Nature's economy; nothing is isolated or lost; even in falling like rotted fruit, men
help to fertilize the tree of life. The Diotima experience is
subordinated to this great process ("Auch wir, auch wir
sind nicht geschieden"); it falls into place, like the Gret-
chen episode in Faust's long life, losing its sharpest ache.
All the dissonances of the world are reconciled and har-

monized, all things severed are reunited, taken up into the one eternal, glowing life.

This concluding picture of serenity, however, is clearly marked at beginning and end ("so dacht' ich," II, 122, 19; 124, 11) as an attitude and condition of the past in a distant land, of the Hyperion who had then completed the series of experiences which the letters narrate. We must turn back to the beginning of the novel to learn the attitude and condition of the *present* Hyperion after he has returned from Germany (where he had the last of those experiences) and assumed, we must infer, his role of *Eremit*. In these *present*-tense opening letters we find him indeed addicted to Nature, on his cherished "Vaterlandsboden," and no human figures appear in the landscape. Yet he is anything but the serene and reconciled individual the last letter had shown. The very opening sentence speaks of sorrow as well as joy that his homeland still brings him. He should have been here, he feels, a thousand years earlier. To be a Greek today is to be buried alive, thrown into a morass, throttled with a dog's collar. He has not got over his resentment at "die weisen Herren" in Germany who gave him such bad counsel. His heart is still starved, assailed, vexed a thousandfold (end of first letter).

In beautiful, poetic language he voices, in the second letter, his creed of union with all living things, "Eines zu seyn mit Allem, was lebt." Having stated this creed, however, he admits at once that he cannot live up to it: "Auf dieser Höhe steh' ich oft. . . . Aber ein Moment des Besinnens wirft mich hinab"; he is nowise bettered, the "ewigeinige Welt" is gone, Nature is alien and incomprehensible, he is alone. And for this unhappy issue he blames mind and thought—though he had earlier regarded these as helpful powers reconciling us with experience: "am

Ende söhnet der Geist mit allem uns aus" (II, 21).[1] If we are to picture Hyperion now as isolated, alienated from his surroundings, a plant uprooted from Nature's garden to wither in the heat (I, 11/12), then we must conclude that the rapturous peace professed at the end of the novel, and earlier in this very letter, is of no permanence.

These first two letters deserve to be given special weight because they reflect the hero's state before he has begun his autobiography and come under the emotional spell of any particular revived memories. After all he has come through, Hyperion, as he embarks (in the third letter) on the story of his life, still speaks of his harassed soul ("angefochtenes Wesen") taking refuge in recollections of childhood and its unquestioning faith; now, when he thinks he has discerned truth, he fears it is only a subjective illusion: he dreams of touching God's hand, only to awake and find himself clutching his own fingers.[2]

[1] At another time, however (after the break with Alabanda), he had shrewdly observed that our thinking itself is colored by our emotions and conforms to the erring heart: "Das eben . . . ist das Traurige, daß unser Geist so gerne die Gestalt des irren Herzens annimmt, . . . daß der Gedanke, der die Schmerzen heilen sollte, selber krank wird." And it seems to be Hölderlin recognizing the special peril of the superior, the artistic individual—in whom the emotional nature is as strong as the intellectual—when Hyperion continues: "das ist die Klippe für die Lieblinge des Himmels, daß ihre Liebe mächtig ist und zart, wie ihr Geist, daß ihres Herzens Woogen stärker oft und schneller sich regen, wie der Trident, womit der Meergott sie beherrscht" (I, 67 f.).

[2] In a later passage, ascribed by Hyperion to his earlier self, there is the suggestion that our gods may be only the product of the pressure of opposing Fate on the human mind: "das eben macht die schönen Träume . . . und . . . Phantome, . . . das schafft dem Menschen sein Elysium und seine Götter, daß seines Lebens Linie nicht gerad ausgeht, . . . und eine fremde Macht dem Fliehenden in den Weg sich wirft." The gods die when our religious urge dies: "Aber dennoch stirbt der Trieb in unserer Brust, und mit ihm unsre Götter und ihr Himmel" (I, 71). In his Athens lecture, Hyperion speaks of the gods as an objectivation of human ideality: "Er

In short, these first three numbers show the present, letter-writing Hyperion as far from settled and assured. And the evidences of his *"un*aufgelöste Dissonanzen" continue. At the beginning of the fifth letter, he sees himself as a peaceless ghost returned from Acheron to haunt the deserted scenes of his youth. In his new and final abode, the island of Salamis (beginning with the twelfth letter), he seems to have reached a calmer state; but his emotional stress can still become too great and need relief (I, 83, 10 ff.), and he must wait a long time for the composure and strength to continue his tale (I, 85, 8 f.). Such terms as he has come to with life do not include any relation to his fellow-men; the hermit seems at the end completely isolated. His peace with the "All" does not extend to human beings.

There is a deep contradiction between the concepts of pantheism and hermithood. For if divinity is everywhere, if all things, including Man, partake of it (and Hyperion, as well as Hölderlin in his poems, affirms the "Gott in uns"), why should one flee the world and commune with Nature exclusively? In a later letter, Hyperion declares that the soul, if it puts away mortal experiences "und allein nur lebt in heiliger Ruhe," is in an unnatural state, like a leafless tree or a hairless head (II, 20). But "living in solitude and holy quiet" is a very definition of hermitdom, which, by implication, is here condemned. It is a solution, moreover, hardly in Diotima's spirit or intent.

In the twenty-first letter, Hyperion tells us what Diotima was to him (and we seem to hear the voice of Hölderlin lamenting his own loss): "O ich wär' ein glüklicher, ein

---

will sich selber fühlen, darum stellt er seine Schönheit gegenüber sich. So gab der Mensch sich seine Götter," etc. (I, 141, 19 ff.). I do not believe that this aspect of Hölderlin's complex religious thought has been much noted.

treflicher Mensch geworden mit ihr!" (I, 105). But all this is gone; he is desolate and completely lost without her; his inner and outer world lack all meaning and purpose. The pantheistic belief in survival in Nature, in which he had seemed to agree so fully with her, is not yet his.

The twenty-third letter, with its agonized reopening of the old wound, shows him still unreconciled to his tragic bereavement and still haunted by the urge to suicide; we should, I think, read this in the lines, reminiscent of Hero and Leander, in which he would beg the raging sea to cast him on the dead Diotima's shore: "in die tobende See will ich mich werfen, und ihre Wooge bitten, daß sie [todt] an Diotima's Gestade mich wirft!" Though he feels that it would be more heroic thus "sich zu befreien auf immer," he resigns himself to palliatives, but they do not make him "zufrieden" (I. 107, 10 f., 13 ff.). He finds no refuge from life's adversity but to bury his heart and wrap himself in the memory of happier times (I, 110, 15 ff.).

Hyperion appears in the novel as an inwardly unsure and impressionable person. He has flashes of insight, and his utterances are often impressive, but they are always in some way conditioned and not clearly committing. Thus in the early letter already referred to (the eighth), he recognizes opposition, contrariety, as a necessary condition for Man's achievement, and vivifies his recognition with an image: "Des Herzens Wooge schäumte nicht so schön empor, und würde Geist, wenn nicht der alte stumme Fels, das Schiksaal, ihr entgegenstünde" (I, 71). But this entire meditation is assigned to the past: it is introduced by "fragt' ich oft" (I, 70, 17) and terminated by "So träumt' ich hin" (I, 72, 11); in any case, it has little relevance to a hermit's life. On the other hand, in a late letter (the third from the last) there is a profound passage to which Lawrence Ryan attaches great importance as containing Hyperion's "abschließende Stellungnahme" and the final "Auflösung der Dissonanzen" (*op. cit.,* pp. 221, 223). At this point, after quoting Notara's last letter, Hyperion interposes a question to Bellarmin: "und du fragst, . . . wie jezt mir ist, indem ich diß erzähle?" and replies that he is "ruhig," for he asks no better lot than the gods'. They, and all beings, must suffer, the more deeply the better they are; even divine Nature suffers. But bliss exempt from suffering would be sleep, and without death there would be no life. One cannot be forever like a slumbering child (this specifically renounces the immature position of the *Schiksaalslied* with its myth of the non-suffering gods, "schiksaallos, wie der schlafende Säugling"). Suffering, *Schmerz,* deserves to be cherished by Man; it is his only fit companion and guide to higher things (II, 106, 11–107, 5).

Mr. Ryan (p. 106) refers to this passage as standing "am Endpunkt des Erzählens." But the point is, it stands at some distance from the end. What we find at the end instead is a seeming peace-in-Nature which, however, is reported of a bygone time and a transient foreign situation. Is not the profound passage just quoted another momentary insight of Hyperion's ("jezt, . . . indem ich diß erzähle"), under the impact of Diotima's death and her sublime testament which he has just finished relating, reliving? He has been *ruhig* before (e.g., I, 69,11; I, 73,7; II, 21,1 ff.)—but not for long. The "Ruhe" and "Bescheidung" claimed for him now are belied further on in this same letter by his utter despondency, self-condemnation, and thoughts of suicide (II, 108, 10 ff.; 109, 8–11, 18). And then follows, so unhappily placed after this broad and deep view (of II, 106/107), the bitter penultimate letter with its vehement outburst against the Germans.

The actual ending (the sixtieth letter) is magnificent as poetry, but it leaves some questions unanswered. In language of exquisite melody and imagery it testifies to the productive power of surmounted sorrow: "daß eine neue Seeligkeit dem Herzen aufgeht, wenn es aushält und die Mitternacht des Grams durchduldet, und daß, wie Nachtigallgesang im Dunkeln, göttlich erst in tiefem Laid das Lebenslied der Welt uns tönt" (II, 119, 11 ff.). But by being immediately attached ("Denn . . .") to a Wertheresque *Naturbegeisterung,* this profound declaration is narrowed and weakened. If it were not such a superlatively beautiful (German) spring, would Hyperion's faith still hold, would he still experience the comforting epiphany of Diotima? What that experience has led to is not quite what she had wished for him, but rather a renouncing of that wish, a turning away from "die kalte Nacht der Menschen" (II, 122, 15), a retreat into the private idyl she had opposed (I, 156, 11 ff.). And even this idyl proves, as we learned from the opening letters, to be not free from relapses.

In her last letter, Diotima confirms the fact that Hyperion has not won fame nor marital happiness: "Dir ist dein Lorbeer nicht gereift und deine Myrthen verblühten." Instead, he is to become "Priester . . . der göttlichen Natur" (II, 104)—a mission which could well be combined with that of "Erzieher unsers Volks," which she had wished for him (I, 159, 20). But the Hermit has no contact with a "Volk," and if he preaches a religion of Nature it is only by letter to a single, distant correspondent. At the end he has attained for himself "den Olymp des Göttlichschönen" in Nature, but he has abandoned the attempt "dahin mein Volk zu führen" (II, 8/9).

Diotima's concluding words, "die dichterischen Tage

keimen dir schon" (II, 104, 12 f.), have been taken to mean that Hyperion is to become a poet.[3] But it seems to me that "dichterische Tage" means rather a higher, consecrated life [4] as priest of the creed of return to Nature, not poetic production in the technical sense. There is no evidence of a special poet's capacity in Hyperion (the *Schiksaalslied* is not original with him), and nothing in Diotima's letters indicates that she expects him to emerge as a poet. The whole emphasis of her present sentence, after acknowledging his failure to win laurel and myrtle, is on his consequent ("denn . . .") true mission as "Priester der göttlichen Natur," with which, as the "und" shows, the anticipated "dichterischen Tage" are connected and identified. Moreover, would not Hölderlin, had he intended a culmination of such importance, compositionally and personally, as Hyperion's becoming a poet, have made this clear and emphatic?

The final words of the novel, "So dacht' ich. Nächstens mehr," look two ways, backwards and forwards. They wind up the past, and they hint at the future; but they tell us nothing about the present. The last two enigmatic words relate, not to the story—for that is finished—but to its framework. They could be taken simply as a finial of the letter fiction, saying, "I'll be writing to you again." Beissner's lengthy note (StA 3, pp. 488–490) does not really explain them. In any case, they leave further communication open, and contemporary and later critics who saw in these

---

[3] L. Ryan, *op. cit.,* pp. 227 ff. In his *Friedrich Hölderlin,* 2. Aufl. (Stuttgart, 1967), p. 45, Ryan again declares "das Werden Hyperions zum Dichter" to be the "verstecktes Hauptthema des Romans."

[4] Hölderlin seems to have taken over here a peculiar Klopstockian nuance of *dichterisch;* see Beissner's note, StA 3, p. 485.

words the promise of a sequel were not wholly unjustified.[5] So discerning a reviewer as the anonymous one of the *Tübingischen gelehrten Anzeigen* of 1801 [6] judged that the plan and course of the second part of *Hyperion* warranted the expectation of a "leztes Heft" which would resolve certain discords in the book—in other words, an intelligent and sympathetic writer familiar with the author felt that not all the "Dissonanzen" has been finally and fully harmonized. A recent writer finds expressed in the final words "the realization that the emotional cycle of the hero, like the historical cycle of birth and destruction, is a continuing, never ending process" [7]—which would seem to call for an "open-end" novel.

Would there be a new turn in the hero's life? Would reflection once again cast him down from the height attained? Was the hermit solution to prove only temporary? Have we been given only the first part, the early-life portion, of a *Bildungsroman?* Was it in this prophetic sense that the hero had been made to say, early in the story, "Guter Junge! sie [die Schülerjahre] sind noch lange nicht vorüber" (I, 15)? Must we conclude that even in this form, as previously in the *Thalia* fragment and other versions, *Hyperion* is an unfinished novel with an unfinished hero?

---

[5] Beissner, StA 3, p. 489, declares categorically that only a person devoid of feeling for "der klaren Gesetzmäßigkeit des künstlerischen Aufbaus, dem feinen Verhältnis der Teile und des Ganzen" could consider a continuation possible. But Emerich and Böhlendorff, both writers and close friends of Hölderlin, expected a third part (see StA 3, p. 318).

[6] Probably Karl Philipp Conz; quoted in full, StA 3, pp. 323 ff.

[7] Emmon Bach, "*Einst* and *Jetzt* in Hölderlin's Works," in *Deutsche Beiträge zur geistigen Überlieferung*, V (1965), p. 152.

IV. *Hyperion as Hero*

Goethe thought that the hero of a novel should be of a passive disposition: "Der Romanenheld muß leidend, wenigstens nicht im hohen Grade wirkend sein." [1] Hyperion more than fulfills this requirement. He is "other-directed" rather than self-directed. His decisions are usually not his own but those of other, stronger individuals: Adamas, Alabanda, Diotima, even Notara. In the mixture of motives that drive him to war, the most prominent are petty jealousy and a feeling of inferiority. He burns and boils with pain at being outdone by his friend: "Mir brannte das Gesicht vor Schaam, mir kochte das Herz, wie heiße Quellen, . . . so schmerzt' es mich, überflogen zu seyn von Alabanda, überwunden auf immer" (II, 6/7), and he grasps at once at the other's suggestion. He is touched on the quick when Diotima tells him he is not born for violent action; he calls her a sophist, when it is he who is one, for he shifts his argument (II, 8). He admits that his decision is com-

[1] *Wilhelm Meisters Lehrjahre*, 2. Teil, 5. Buch, 7. Kapitel.

[39]

pulsive, not voluntary: ". . . ich muß! Ich wähle nicht, ich sinne nicht. Eine Macht ist in mir und ich weiß nicht, ob ich es selbst bin, was zu dem Schritte mich treibt" (II, 10). At Athens, he had quickly agreed to Diotima's suggestion that he become an educational leader of his people (after first educating himself); now he is equally quick to abandon this plan at Alabanda's suggestion and join him in the war.[2]

Again and again, Hyperion is represented as irresolute, immature, and suggestible. He accepts Notara's advice about procedure, though it is contrary to his own feeling: "Das war mir nicht recht nach meinem Sinne" (II, 12, 13), later, he accepts Notara's judgment and does not return to Kalaurea, though he feels he could well live there "nach meinem Sinne" (II, 110 f.). There is no evidence of an inner motivation for his trip to Germany late in the story; he simply journeys vaguely northwest, "weil es die Gelegenheit so haben will," and arrives forthwith (no word is expended on the voyage): "So kam ich unter die Deutschen" (II, 111, 112). Disillusionment with German philosophy and German humanity apparently influences his decision to retire from the world. The writing of his story, in the first place, was not undertaken on his own impulse, but in response to an outsider's request (I, 12). The *Schiksaalslied,* so often identified with him, is not his own, but an echo, "meinem Adamas nachgesprochen" (II, 94, 11).

In encounters with his friend Alabanda, Hyperion does not come off with great credit. He is intolerant, ungenerous, and womanish in his reaction to Alabanda's connec-

---

[2] It is interesting to note that Goethe's Werther at one time is minded to undertake war service with a foreign power (am 25. Mai), a project that Hyperion actually carries out.

tion with the "Bund der Nemesis" (I, 55 ff.). Already
nettled by Alabanda's mockery of his earlier effusion, he
forthwith convicts him of guilt by association (though it
turns out that Alabanda is a victim rather than an ally of
the *Bund*) and scents a conspiracy against himself (I, 60 f.).
Alabanda's attitude the following day (I, 62 ff.) is marked
by manly dignity and composure, Hyperion's by arrogance
and hysteria, and it is he who forces a break. When Alabanda writes again, after a long interval, it is to say that he
has removed all obstacles to their reunion (at his own peril,
as appears later) and found a new mission for them both.
Hyperion, however, without a word for his friend's devotion and generosity, sees in the letter only a threat to his
ego, outstripped by Alabanda's enterprise (II, 6 f.).

The immaturity of Hyperion's character appears most
clearly when it is shown in relation to Diotima's. He notes
a change in her (an effect of his misguided military ven-
ture), but is blind to its meaning, considering it merely the
maturing of his "seeliges Kind" (II, 11). When (in the farewell scene) she voices the natural and reasonable wish to
go with him on the campaign, he somewhat grandilo-
quently refers her to her role as priestess of the home. She
accepts his decision with a grief that she tries to hide. He,
not sensing the depth of her feeling, ascribes her tears to
confusion ("Verwirrung") and blames himself for having
made her blush "schaamroth"—as though an immodest
request had been denied (II, 15/16)! In his self-centered
excitement he deems the others cold and blind: "ihr steht
alle so kalt! . . . Diotima!—du siehst nicht!—o wohl dir,
daß du nicht siehst!" She does not retort or expose his
blindness but acquiesces in his departure with forbearing
love: "geh nur, du theures Herz!" He, instead of strength-
ening her with great-hearted thoughts, as she implores him

to do ("rede mit größerem Herzen mir zu!"), adds to her distress with desperate expressions of doom ("Wehe! ... das ist kein Abschied, wo man wiederkehrt")—until Notara protests that his frantic outburst is killing her, who is so gentle and controlled (II, 18). In their last farewell under the stars, she is again the leader, he the follower. She stands on a height of self-conquest and spiritualization which he cannot yet measure, a height at which bodily separation and death lose their meaning and life with all its suffering and joy is seen *sub specie aeternitatis* as deeply good. Hyperion only knows that he "feels different" ("Es ist mir auch jezt anders"), and he takes his cue from her: "Vollendete! ... ich spreche wie du" (II, 19–20).

In his ensuing letters from the field Hyperion often appears self-concerned and unperceptive. He misses the clear signs of approaching death in Diotima's first replies (the forty-third and forty-seventh letters), the ominous "noch" and concern with the end of noble Spartan women.[3] In a weak and selfish way he pours out his fears and troubles upon her, who is far away and helpless. He has no comfort for her, but flings her a "Sei selbst dein Trost!" (II, 47). Considering himself disgraced, he decrees arbitrarily (with less reason than Lessing's Tellheim) that their troth must be broken; he decides to join the Russian fleet.

A major reason for the inconclusiveness of the novel is the lability of its hero. Hyperion is the very type of the manic-depressive. It is his nature to fly from one extreme to the other, to be hurled, like Vulcan, but countless times, from heaven to earth (I, 118, 119 f.). One moment he is at the pinnacle of ecstasy, all but divine; the next he is plunged into darkest desolation: "es war mir oft, als läuter-

---

[3] The first three lines of the next letter, however (II, 44, 6–8), I take to be not selfish reproof but bitter irony—a mood rare in Hölderlin and hence not readily recognized.

ten sich und schmelzten die Dinge der Erde, wie Gold, in meinem Feuer zusammen, und ein Göttliches wurde aus ihnen und mir, so tobte in mir die Freude, . . . Aber nicht lange, so war das alles, wie ein Licht, in mir erloschen, und stumm und traurig, wie ein Schatte, saß ich da und suchte das entschwundne Leben" (I, 114 f.). Diotima soon recognizes his "unstet Wesen," the "Ebb und Fluth" [4] of his "ruheloses Herz" (I, 110, 103), and she explains to him "warum so schröklich Freude und Laid dir wechselt" (I, 119). This echoes the dichotomy in the opening sentence of the novel, and indeed from first to last we find antithetical phrases that express Hyperion's emotional "swing": "Steigen" and "Sinken," "Seeligkeit" and "Trauer," "Streit" and "Einklang" (I, 84), "Größe" and "Demuth," "Lust" and "Trauer" (I, 99), "Entzüken" and "Schmerz," "Tod der Freude" and "Tod der Trauer" (I, 106), "Leiden" and "Freudigkeit" (II, 19), "Wonne" and "Schmerz" (II, 53), and many more.

Labile and suggestible as he is, Hyperion has moments of insight, but on the whole he fails to sense Diotima's quality and destructibleness. After the debacle of Misistra he writes in unrestrained terms of desperation. It argues a shallowness in his own nature that he fails to perceive the depth of hers, that he does not imagine how deeply she will take what for him are momentary heroics of self-pity. She overestimates his tragedy and his greatness (II, 68–73), he underestimates hers. Because her experience and love are deeper than his, she must suffer more; it is under the impact of her fate that it will later dawn on him how all life must suffer, "und je treflicher es ist, je tiefer!" (II, 106).

The letter in which Hyperion breaks off their engage-

---

[4] There is some self-portraiture in this, as Hölderlin's letters prove, e.g., one to Neuffer, 8. November 1790: "Ich bin zum Stoiker ewig verdorben. Das seh' ich wol. Ewig Ebb' und Fluth" (StA 6, Nr. 35, lines 13 f.).

ment is full of self-pity but has no pity for Diotima, holds out no hope for her, in fact shows her there is no hope. He is insulting as well as patronizing when he writes "du fändest ewig keinen Frieden bei Hyperion, du müßtest untreu werden und das will ich dir ersparen" (II, 51). Having courted her compassion and wrung her heart, he adds "but don't listen to me!": "aber höre das nicht! ich bitte dich, achte das nicht!" (II, 52, 3 ff.). At the end, he hints at suicide—for the loss of Greece (II, 52, 8–10)!

In the following letter, in which the suicide note becomes dominant, the "Erdenrund" he declares he can dispense with, the "Außendinge" he is ready to shake off (II, 54, 1 f., 10 f.) , include her! As a last turn of the screw, he torments her broken heart with the gratuitous notion that his poor body will go unburied (II, 55), so that (unlike Schiller's Thekla) she cannot even visit her lover's grave! *He* gets relief by writing all these things, but he does not consider what reading them must do to *her*. Then, having terrified her with his dark threats, he leaves her for months without news (II, 67, 10 f.)! Here again the letter business becomes extremely questionable.

To Alabanda, Hyperion confesses ruefully that he had meant to desert him by seeking a violent end in battle; "war das nicht herzlos? rasend?" he asks, and adds, as an afterthought, "ach und meine Diotima!" and mentions his two letters to her. Alabanda's shocked reaction makes him realize that it was also somewhat *herzlos* to write as he did to her. With easy optimism, however, he persuades himself that a specially accelerated letter will set matters right and that *he* can still be happy with his "angel." [5]

Meanwhile Diotima has written, and Hyperion, moved by her loyal acquiescence in his desperate steps, senses at

---

[5] II, 65–66; "Engel" also II, 16, 4. "Einen Engel!" says Werther, "Pfui! das sagt jeder von der Seinigen, nicht wahr?" (am 16. Junius).

last how greatly she has changed her nature to adjust to his (II, 73/74). He, on the other hand, feels "ich bin dir jezt dafür in deinem Eigensten um so ähnlicher geworden" (II, 75). Thus, in ironical reversal, the lovers have to some extent exchanged places. But his assimilation is much less radical than hers, and the solution he proposes and elaborates so enticingly: retreat to an idyllic vale of the Alps or Pyrenees (II, 76 f.), is a banal expedient unworthy of her depth. And he fears, with good reason, that it may be too late even for this. The latter part of his letter is full of misgivings, and it cannot truly comfort Diotima to be told that she is the last possession he has salvaged from the ruin of his life, the last asylum from which he dreads to be driven (II, 78, 17–79, 3). Having dispatched this letter, nevertheless, he is "ziemlich sorglos" (II, 79, 12) again, influenced by Alabanda's hopefulness. He assumes that things will be as before and that he can soon take Diotima, her mother, and Alabanda with him into a new life! Little does he dream that he is soon to lose his friend and his beloved, both of them ultimately victims of their loyalty to him.

In the early days of their friendship, Hyperion and Alabanda had vied with each other in high-sounding vows to judge and cleanse the wretched world—wholly in "Gedanken" and "kolossalischen Entwürfen" (I, 45), a purely mental exercise. Even what action they imagined depended on imaginary assistants: "O! zünde mir einer die Fakel an . . . ! die Mine bereite mir einer, daß ich . . . !" (I, 48). When they meet again in the war, they continue in this vein. Hyperion proclaims his resolve to restore the glory of a race of whom even Jupiter and Apollo were only copies. He calls the Ionian heaven and earth to witness his vow: "ich will es länger nicht dulden!" Alabanda bids the very sun watch their progress. "Es entzündete einer den andern" (II, 28)—in a fire of mere words. There is so little substance in these tirades, so little staying power in this rhetorical patriotism, that after two or three unsuccessful battles, neither again lifts a finger in his country's cause; Alabanda hands himself over to his secret society for execution, while Hyperion turns back to his private life, only to find it broken beyond repair.

The hermit who at the end secedes from the world to relive his past and commune with Nature is a maimed man. He has caught only part of the meaning of Diotima's life and death. He has failed of the career of social usefulness she had envisioned for him. In the heyday of their love, when he would have been content to withdraw to his "seelige Insel," ignoring the world's shipwreck (I, 156, 11 f.), she had showed him a greater challenge: "denkst du wirklich, daß du nun am Ende seyst? Willst du dich verschließen in den Himmel deiner Liebe, und die Welt, die deiner bedürfte, verdorren und erkalten lassen unter dir?" She had begged him to go to Athens and look at the simple *Menschen* there, his fellow-Greeks: "kannst du sagen, ich schäme mich dieses Stoffs? . . . Kannst du dein Herz abwenden von den Bedürftigen? Sie sind nicht schlimm, sie haben dir nichts zu laide gethan!" (I, 157–158)—doubtless a truer picture of the Greeks than the fratricidal horde at Misistra that Hölderlin took over [6] from

---

[6] See StA 3, pp. 476 f. — It is possible too that Goethe's *Götz von Berlichingen* had some influence on the military operations in *Hyperion*. The hero's disillusionment in the undisciplined mountaineers he leads is like Götz's in his lawless peasants. The one speaks bitterly of his men as "Mordbrenner" and "Hunde" (*Götz*, Act V, Sc. 5), the other of "die Barbaren, an deren Spize ich war" (*Hyp.*, II, 45). The faithless troops, when they encounter real enemy resistance, are deservedly defeated (V, 5; II, 46). Alabanda, like Götz's Georg, just escapes being captured with the miscreants (V, 14; II, 47). Alabanda's exultant "es soll ein ziemlich Feuer werden" (II, 27) sounds like an echo of Metzler's grim "Wird ein hübsch Feuerchen geben" (V, 1).

a falsifying German translation of a French travel book. Of Diotima's mature social conscience there is little trace in Hyperion. After the brief and inglorious campaign, he washes his hands of the Greeks, and *Menschen* do not figure in his story again.

V. *Diotima*

The real hero of this novel is a heroine: not the unfinished
and unclarified Hyperion but Diotima, the only completely
delineated character in the book. Her life, like that of a
sublime figure of Schiller's, "liegt faltenlos und leuchtend
ausgebreitet." She too comes out of "des Ideales Reich."
Beginning as the palest abstraction of womanhood, Melite,
in the earliest version, this conception was strangely cor-
roborated and enriched by experience [1] until it became as
real a person as Hölderlin's reticent lyrical art could create.

Of physical love and sexual passion there is hardly a
hint in the lovers' relationship. At the moment of her
frank and full avowal of love, Diotima looks upon Hyperion "in voller Herzenslust," embraces him "in kühner

---

[1] Diotima's death, the necessity of which in the novel Susette apparently did not agree to (see StA 6, No. 198, lines 2–4) and its effect on
Hyperion were to find an uncanny parallel in Hölderlin's real life. The
broken poet, too, in his Homburg refuge was to be near to "Diotima's
Grab" (I, 106).

heiliger Freude," and kisses his brow, lips, and bare breast
(I, 135, 15 ff.). But this, like Hyperion's transports as he
holds her above the cliff (I, 98, 6 ff.), is tender, admiring
affection and not desire, *Seelenfreundschaft* and not *Liebes-
leidenschaft*. It is like Hölderlin's own relation to Susette
Gontard: "eine ewige fröhliche heilige Freundschaft mit
einem Wesen, das sich recht in diß arme geist- und ord-
nungslose Jahrhundert verirrt hat." [2] Of the many forms of
love between man and woman, *Hyperion* is a monument
to the most spiritual and hence imperishable.

Diotima embodies the ideal toward which the whole
book tends. She is the very spirit of selflessness. She has
from the beginning that "seelige Selbstvergessenheit" (I,
10, 13 f.) without which Man cannot return to the divine
universe of Nature, his first and his final home (II, 101,
14 ff.). In the twentieth letter, taking up an equivocal observation by Hyperion, Diotima states simply but with
utter conviction her pantheistic faith in Nature: that we
are all, in all eternity, "Kinder des Hauses" and cannot be
lost from its great household. Hyperion echoes her view in
many more words, and later he tries to live by it, but it is
doubtful whether at the end he can say so simply for himself "Ich vertraue der Natur" (I, 102 f.).

Diotima's original nature and life are marked by the
serenity and self-sufficiency which Hölderlin constantly
attributes to the divine. She is completely "bedürfnißlos"
and "göttlichgenügsam," as peaceful as the strand of
blessed isles before the waves of Hyperion's restless spirit
begin to beat upon them (I, 103). But she does not deny
herself to love for the sake of preserving her paradise.

She becomes her lover's counselor and guide, the
source of his deepest wisdom as well as highest happiness.

[2] Letter of February 16, 1797, to Neuffer; StA 6, No. 136, lines 9–11.

In what he fitly calls a "Seelengespräch" (I, 123, 11) she diagnoses his character and fate, which she has reason to say she understands better than he (I, 118–121). Again and again it is she who speaks prophetic and directive wisdom, which he accepts, even though late and perhaps not permanently. He learns equanimity and *Sammlung* from her: "Schon lange war unter Diotima's Einfluß mehr Gleichgewicht in meine Seele gekommen; heute [on the great day in Athens] fühlt' ich es dreifach rein, und die zerstreuten schwärmenden Kräfte waren all in Eine goldne Mitte versammelt" (I, 137). He learns from her to be less talkative: "meine Diotima hatte mich so einsylbig gemacht" (I, 111). She inspirits him: "Mein ganzes Wesen richtete sich auf, da ich einmal wieder mit Diotima allein mich sah" (I, 154, 11 f.). In the gathering at Athens, he is by far the most vocal, but she exercises a quiet guidance, discerning his trouble with a clear eye and showing him the larger view (I, 156, 16 ff.). She tells him frankly when his utterance passes into mere rhetoric and improvisation: "Guter Hyperion! . . . es ist Zeit, daß du weggehst; . . . du suchst dir umsonst mit Einfällen zu helfen" (I, 154).

Her first reaction to Alabanda's proposal of military activity shows her to be maturer and wiser than her lover. But she generously takes his proud and eloquent patriotism at full value and, submerging her wishes and doubts, urges him to do what his heart craves. She honors his exaltation: "Ach! wenn du so bist, hab' ich keine Macht, kein Recht auf dich!" (II, 10). With a simple heroism that contrasts with his magniloquence, she declares "Handle du; ich will es tragen" (II, 10).[3] The following letter shows the begin-

[3] This is a kind of anticipation of Hebbel's formulation "Durch Dulden Thun: Idee des Weibes" (*Tagebücher*, ed. Werner, I, p. 338, No. 1516).

ning of her apotheosis. An inner fire begins to consume her like a sacrifice; spiritual growth keeps pace with physical attrition. Quietly, piously, without self-pity, she assumes her tragic fate.

The forty-third letter reveals her brave and devoted character and her kinship with Nature. It begins with an implied figure: she gathers last vitality in the open and brings it like a gift of flowers to her beloved: "In holder Februarluft hab' ich Leben gesammelt und bringe das gesammelte dir" (II, 31). She is sister to "der Pflanzenwelt, der reinen, immergleichen, wo alles trauert und sich wieder freut zu seiner Zeit. . . . Warum gehn wir denn die stillen Lebenswege nicht auch?" (II, 31/32). (In one of his early observations, the hermit echoes this longing: "Alles altert und verjüngt sich wieder. Warum sind wir ausgenommen vom schönen Kreislauf der Natur?" I, 27). Diotima's letter is a love song; by the hand of loving memory she raises herself from despondency to joy as she writes. This is a triumph of the spirit, a very feminine heroism. But the foreboding "noch" (II, 31, 16 f.) and other overtones seem lost on her preoccupied lover. He holds out only public satisfactions to her (II, 30/31), which will not stay the wilting of her private happiness and life.

Diotima's loyal love does not for a moment cloud her intelligence. When she reads Hyperion's letter breaking off their connection because of his alleged unworthiness, she at once puts her finger on the real reason, and accepts it: "O es ist so ganz natürlich, daß du nimmer lieben willst, weil deine größern Wünsche verschmachten" (II, 67 f.). She had realized almost from the start that she could only be second-best in his heart: "Ich wußte es bald: ich konnte dir nicht Alles seyn" (II, 68). She knew that he loved humanity more (I, 121, 3 ff.) and Greece more (II, 72, 14 f.), and that to understand him and love him, who is "im Grunde trostlos," was to become infected with his incurable tragedy (II, 68). This fate she took upon herself, obeying the law of love, the law of Goethe's Amyntas: "Wer sich der Liebe vertraut, hält er sein Leben zu Rat?"

Seeing more clearly and feeling more deeply than Hyperion, Diotima could have led and dominated in their relationship. Instead, she denies her own original nature to follow him in his alien course. She sees the change in him and its threat to their love; "Aber wandle nur zu! Ich folge dir," she declares; even if he should come to hate her, she would try to follow him in that (II, 42). The final paragraph, wistfully framed by "Lebewohl," sums up well the heroic yet feminine loyalty of the whole letter: her loving wish for his self-fulfillment, her recognition of the great concerns of war and peace, justice and natural law, and the new commonwealth (Gemeinde) which she will not live to see; and at the same time her womanly anxiety for peace and the preservation of frail and precious things (II, 43 f.).

In loving identification, Diotima takes on Hyperion's indignation and despair: "ich bin das sanfte Mädchen nicht mehr. . . . Die Entrüstung treibt mich aufwärts, daß ich kaum zur Erde sehen mag und unablässig zittert mein belaidigtes Herz" (II, 72) . She resigns her natural right to marriage and children; she gives up all claim to the man for love of whom she has made so many sacrifices (II, 73).

All the heart-wringing pathos that Hölderlin's elegiac genius could summon is put into Diotima's long last letter: the poignant sadness of final farewell; the weary, failing heart revisiting for the last time scenes of bygone happiness; she, "die Naturverbundene," taking leave of the trees and flowers that were her friends and kindred. It is an appealing touch in her portrait that for all her lofty phi-

losophy of immortality she shrinks like a frightened bird
from the sight of the beautiful earth that she must leave
(II, 98). With generous solicitude she anticipates and seeks
to disarm even Hyperion's self-reproach over her fate (II,
99). Yet her own summary (II, 100, 5–18) makes it plain
that he caused her death.[4] He drew her out of her natural
world and kindled in her his own dangerous fire, but then,
instead of giving her a new anchorage in life, pointed the
way out of it. When the public interests that were more important to him than his love failed him after a brief trial,
he declared himself through with life and set on suicide.
This resolve, again ephemeral for him, robbed her existence of meaning and broke her spirit. She has given up
everything for him, he nothing for her. She perishes, he
survives. Hers is the major tragedy in the book; the tragedy
of his frustrated life is the minor one. She has by far the
greater integrity of character. Alabanda, who never meets
her, senses that she is "um und um so innig Eines . . . , Ein
göttlich ungetheiltes Leben" and needs to be loved whole-
heartedly if at all (II, 81); life denies her this. Characteristically, her last thought, the last vision that fills her dying
eye, is that of her Hyperion in his future glory (II, 104).
Diotima is selfless love to her last breath.

She is also the spirit of loving wisdom. Of more than
one insight Hyperion could say to her "Ich hab' es von dir"
(I, 141, 13). When, near the end of his account, he assures
us he has reached calm ("ich bin ruhig," II, 106, 13), it is
in a mood of modesty and gratefulness that is Diotima's,
not originally his, a pious acceptance of that suffering from
which even the gods are not exempt. Of the universality of
Leiden and its requisiteness to life he had had a glimpse—
a conditioned one, as we saw—when he spoke of the rock

---

[4] He admits this later: II, 109, 8–11.

of fate that forced the heart's tide to rise in splendor (I, 71). Now, thanks to Diotima, his understanding is deepened. Her fate had opened his eyes to the tragedy inherent in all existence: even the highest beauty and divinity must humble itself and share the mortality of all mortal creatures (II, 5). Now he says "ich will nichts bessers haben, als die Götter. Muß nicht alles leiden? Und je treflicher es ist, je tiefer!" (II, 106).

What the *Schiksaalslied* had represented as the enviable lot of the gods: to be like a sleeping infant, shielded from fate and change, is now depreciated: "Solltest du ewig seyn, wie ein Kind und schlummern, dem Nichts gleich? den Sieg entbehren?" (II, 106). But already Diotima had said this when in a spirit of love she had seen beyond love and reproved his immature isolationism: "Es giebt eine Zeit der Liebe, . . . wie es eine Zeit giebt, in der glüklichen Wiege zu leben. Aber das Leben selber treibt uns heraus" (I, 156). When Hyperion says "ohne Tod ist kein Leben" (II, 106, 17), he is echoing Diotima's "führt nicht . . . das Leben den Tod mit sich?" (II, 104, 3). His rhetorical question "Was ist denn der Tod?" (II, 124, 2) reaffirms her "Was ist denn Trennung?" (II, 19, 8 f.). When she says "Sterblichkeit ist Schein" (I, 133) or "Wir trennen uns nur, um inniger einig zu seyn. . . . Wir sterben, um zu leben" (II, 103), she anticipates the thought and imagery of his final insights (II, 123, 16 ff.).

In his quieted mood after the collapse of his military ambitions, the convalescent Hyperion rediscovers the Nature world that is Diotima's: "O heilige Pflanzenwelt! . . . wir streben und sinnen und haben doch dich! . . . Dich will ich lieben, harmlos Leben, Leben des Hains und des Quells" (II, 63 f.). This is a prelude to his final solution that fulfills her prophecy "Die schöne Welt ist mein

Olymp; in diesem wirst du leben, und mit den . . . Göttern der Natur . . . wirst du freudig seyn" (II, 101, 11–13; cf. II, 122, 19 ff.). As she had risen above the patchwork made by "Menschenhände" to attain the life of Nature, "das höher ist, denn alle Gedanken" (II, 102), so he at the end prizes one moment in Nature's peace and beauty above all human reasoning and experiment, above "Jahre voll Gedanken" and "alle Versuche der allesversuchenden Menschen" (II, 121). This last phrase too is originally hers (see II, 101, 17); but whereas she had charitably adjured the gods to take errant mortals back into their Nature home, Hyperion shuts them out and reserves this salvation for himself (II, 122, 15 ff.).

But the deepest of Diotima's wisdom, in which she leads the way for an uncertain Hyperion, is her recognition of change as the fundamental law of life. In the pivotal discussion in Athens, amid the ruins of ancient Greece, Heraclitus's ἓν διάφερον ἑαυτῷ, "das Eine in sich selber unterschiedne" (I, 145, 12 f.), was taken as a definition of the essence of Beauty. It could be taken more broadly as a definition of Life. The problem "wie das ungeschiedene Vollkommene sich in Unterscheidungen darstellt" was seen by Wilhelm Michel as the basic problem of Hölderlin's life.[5] How shall we reconcile unity with diversity, permanence with transiency? The traditional antithesis between Man's lot and the gods' is left merely stated in the *Schiksaalslied*: peacelessness, blind falling through endless time are there pathetically contrasted with fateless, changeless duration (the gods are conventionally conceived as "droben," walking on fleecy clouds, not indwelling in Nature).

Instead of passively accepting this static notion, Dio-

---

[5] Wilhelm Michel, *Das Leben Friedrich Hölderlins* (1963), p. 550.

tima's keen and courageous mind confronts the process underlying existence, and asserts the validity of the temporal beside the eternal. In two luminous paragraphs (II, 103, 12–104, 7) of a prose poetry that exquisitely combines profound thought with beautiful language, in the all-but-last words of her valedictory letter, she sets forth the principle of change, the permanence of life and beauty in change, the necessity of change to their permanence. The stars represent perfection in duration; we represent perfection in transiency: "Beständigkeit haben die Sterne gewählt. . . . Wir stellen im Wechsel das Vollendete dar" (II, 103). Our fleeting lives divide off the great unending "Lebenslied der Welt" into melodies that rise and fall, begin and cease. We are like harp players gathered about the thrones of the undying gods of Nature—the Sun and the stars, Aether and Earth—sharing in our measure their divinity, accompanying and softening with the fugitive grace of our life-songs the awesome grandeur of their vast diapason.

Then the figure varies, though the thought is the same: life is not static; it is a never-ending triumphal procession with which Nature celebrates its continuing victory over death and destruction; and we mortals are the youths and maidens who in joyful if changeful bands garland, as it were, the majestic train.[6] This is an original and poetic elaboration of a thought that is as old as Heraclitus and still valid today, when we know that even the "eternal" stars, the very galaxies, alter and age.

How much of Diotima's wisdom does Hyperion make his own? He tries to follow her in her brave, trusting sur-

[6] Cf. in *Empedokles* the concept of the "geschäfftge Reigentanz" of life with which mortals honor the supreme Spirit (3. Fassung, lines 186–189)—one of the many links from *Hyperion* to Hölderlin's other works.

render to Nature. In the end he feels himself one with earth's waters and flowers and forests, with the sky and its eagles and its kindred Light, all united in an ancient brotherhood of love, alike in essence, however varied in outward form: "Frei sind wir, gleichen uns nicht ängstig von außen; . . . innigst im Innersten gleichen wir uns." He accepts change as the law of all life: "wie sollte nicht wechseln die Weise des Lebens?" (in the last letter, II, 123, 12–16), and his ear catches what Hölderlin elsewhere called "die Göttersprache, das Wechseln und das Werden" (*Der Archipelagus*).

In his discussion of *Der Zeitgeist,* Wilhelm Michel credits that ode with marking a turning-point in Hölderlin's thought and attitude toward life, adding a new, historical dimension to his "Weltschau," and constituting a rueful "Absage an die Hyperion-Haltung." [7] But the very terms Michel uses to characterize this new acceptance of change and human transiency, "das Wechseln der Stunden als die notgedrungene 'Weise des Lebens' zu begreifen," are taken from *Hyperion* (II, 123, 14 f.). They are Hyperion's words, but, as we have seen, they echo the deeper and surer wisdom of Diotima. There, rather than in the not wholly conclusive poem,[8] in her clear insight, however faltering Hyperion's pursuit of it, we can discern a new departure in Hölderlin's philosophy of life.

The uncertainties of the opening letters make us doubt Hyperion's firmness in all these convictions. There is no assurance that he will apply them to life and fulfill Dio-

---

[7] Michel, *Leben* (1963), p. 268.

[8] There is some confusing theocrasy in *Der Zeitgeist* as the new "deity of contemporary events" seems to usurp the role of "Vater Aether," awakening life and mind with his light (middle stanza). Moreover, the poem ends rather negatively. Its chief distinction lies in its opening lines: see Chapter VIII, note 2.

tima's hope of his leadership.[9] The hermit in his isolated hut of boughs who broods over the past, reads in history books, and occasionally fishes in the bay (I, 83, 11 ff.) is not the "große Mensch" and "Erzieher unsers Volks" that she had envisaged (I, 159) nor the "höher Wesen" that Notara at times divined in him (II, 106). What life has taught him he has sequestered from life as a private possession. He has after all retired to his "seelige Insel," though its chief "Seeligkeit," Diotima, is lost.

Why did Hölderlin make Diotima such a fine figure and Hyperion such an imperfect one? One could answer, somewhat facetiously, that the hero of an *Entwicklungsroman* is by hypothesis faulty, in order that he may be improved in the course of the story. But Hyperion seems to have more faults than he needs for such purpose, and the final stage of his "improvement" is not entirely clear. Moreover, *Hyperion* is not simply an *Entwicklungsroman*. It is a subjective and lyrical work, not the product of an "epical" novelist who could create characters detached from his personal experience. Its hero is to a high degree a critical self-portrait, its heroine an adoring idealization. *Hyperion* is a love song consecrated to the poet's three loves: Nature, Greece, and Diotima; and the dearest of these is she, in whom—the *Athenerinn,* the sister of trees and flowers—all three loves meet. For Hölderlin, she became fused with the Diotima of his own life, as his novel became a testimony to their essential existence ("vom Leben unseres Lebens") and a thanksgiving ("Dank") for

[9] Diotima's hope for Hyperion's future accomplishment was so strong and vivid that she expresses it in the past indicative as though it had been realized (II, 70, 10–72, 7). This has misled some readers, and even Hölderlin scholars, though they should have noted the concluding "Stille! Stille! Es war mein schönster Traum."

her.[10] The beloved woman above all is glorified, and it is her lover who tells her story, in all modesty and self-disparagement. It is the same spirit that informs many a love poem of Hölderlin's and that makes *Hyperion* the close forerunner of his immortal "Liebeselegie," *Menons Klagen um Diotima.*

---

[10] StA 6, No. 198, lines 5 ff. The letter, of autumn 1799, accompanied his gift copy of volume two to her; see Adolf Beck's note, StA 6, p. 987.

VI. *Epical and Lyrical*

Hölderlin's living Diotima, Susette Gontard, who was involved in *Hyperion* in more than one sense,[1] wrote to the
author, apropos of her reading of novels: "[Dabei] fällt
mir ein, daß Du Deinen lieben Hyperion auch einen
Roman nennst, ich denke mir aber immer dabey ein
schönes Gedicht." [2] Her feeling for the lyrical quality of
Hyperion was soon confirmed more professionally by the
anonymous reviewer (probably Conz) of the *Tübingische
gelehrten Anzeigen,* who judged: "Das Ganze ist, nach
unsrer Ansicht, mehr ein Poëm, als ein Roman: ein
lyrisches Gedicht von größerer Ausdehnung könnte man
es nennen." For, the reviewer points out, it develops no

[1] Hölderlin's letter to her (actually an uncompleted draft, autumn
1799), which Beissner rightly calls "das ergreifendste Dokument zur
Entstehungsgeschichte des Hyperion" (StA 3, p. 318, 3 ff.), attests a con-
sultative participation, as well as inspiration, for "unsern Hyperion" (StA
6, No. 198, esp. lines 1–11).

[2] *Die Briefe der Diotima,* ed. Viëtor (Leipzig, 1922), p. 30; letter of
March 19, 1799.

"Hauptbegebenheit" but rather the individuality of one character. What little action there is serves to motivate an "innere Handlung." As a novel hero Hyperion would seem too "überschwänglich" or "überspannt," too passive, even for Goethe's requirement; this is easier to forgive if we consider him "gleichsam als das Substitut für den lyrischen Dichter," expressing *his* feelings. Hence also, as one would not expect in a novel, the few minor characters are not sufficiently distinct from the main figure, but utter the same views in the same language.[3]

This last point is surely an overstatement in the otherwise discerning and eminently tactful review. It is true that there is a rather uniform "high style" for all persons, even the dubious delegates of the "Bund der Nemesis"; but what the reviewer misses could perhaps be more closely defined as a dramatic opposition in the characters. Years later, Eduard Mörike, in a brief and impatient expostulation in a private letter, spoke of *Hyperion* as a series of supreme lyrics trying anxiously to be a novel with a plot: "lauter einzelne, unvergleichlich wahre und schöne Lyrika, ängstlich auf eine Handlung übergetragen."[4] Achim von Arnim (in a letter to the Grimm brothers in 1817) declared this novel "die herrlichste aller Elegien," and Walther Rehm, quoting him, for his part characterized it as "eine heroische Elegie."[5] H. H. Borcherdt saw in it an "elegische Grundhaltung, die dem Werk einen lyrischen Charakter verleiht."[6] One could cite other writers from Hölderlin's

[3] The review, published January 12, 1801, is reprinted in StA 3, pp. 323 ff.

[4] Letter of May 21, 1832, to Mährlen. Mörike's *Briefe*, ed. Seebass, Tübingen n.d., p. 344.

[5] W. Rehm, *Orpheus* (Düsseldorf, 1950), pp. 311, 325.

[6] H. H. Borcherdt, *Der Roman der Goethezeit* (Urach/Stuttgart [1949]), pp. 360 f.

time to ours who ascribe a lyrical character to *Hyperion,* without, however, demonstrating it in detail.

On the other hand, Friedrich Beissner, the leading Hölderlin authority and expert editor of the definitive *Stuttgarter Ausgabe,* contends that this so-called "lyrical" aspect of the novel has been exaggerated, to the neglect of its objective epical quality.[7] Beissner's pupil, Lawrence Ryan, in his learned and methodical monograph, strongly seconds this opinion, likewise putting "lyrical" into skeptical quotation marks and declaring that this conception has always stood in the way of a proper understanding of the novel and its "streng durchgehaltenes, . . . episches Kompositionsprinzip." [8] It seems to me, on the contrary, that a re-examination of *Hyperion* can only substantiate its lyrical character with fresh evidence.

To call *Hyperion* a novel is only an approximate classification. Its publisher, Cotta, announced it as a "Roman," but added that its author, a young man "von Genie und Talenten," "schlug einen eigenen Weg ein." [9] What Hölderlin's nature or genius inclined to, what by gift or talent he was capable of, was lyrical utterance, whether in verse or prose. His attempted drama, *Empedokles,* is proof of this fact.[10] In his hands a novel could not be an objective, realistic account of persons, places, ideas, and events held together by a clear and cogent plot; rather, all these things would be apprehended in personal, emotional, even musical terms and conveyed in a rhythmical, euphonious

[7] E.g., StA 3, p. 430, 5 ff.—It should be pointed out that in the following discussion I also use "epic(al)" in the broader German sense.

[8] L. Ryan, *Hölderlins "Hyperion"* (1965), p. 1 and passim.

[9] Quoted in StA 3, p. 312, 15 f.

[10] In *Grund zum Empedokles,* Hölderlin discusses his project under the apt rubric of "die tragische Ode" (StA 4, p. 149, 2, and passim).

language that is not a bare vehicle of narration but a medium, beautiful in itself, for feeling and vision. If we expected to find in *Hyperion* "the stirring story of a heroic fight to found a new state," we should be deeply disappointed, and the "lyrical and contemplative strain" must indeed appear to "break the force of the book." [11] Only if we recognize this lyrical quality as the formative essence of the book do its meaning and value become fully evident. Its many pages that "belong to the most magnificent lyrical prose in the German language" [12] are not a surface adornment but the natural expression of a great lyric poet. Friedrich Theodor Vischer's judgment, despite its deprecating tone, remains valid: Hölderlin was for him "ein voller, ein wahrhaft großer Dichter als Lyriker, wenn auch nur als Lyriker." [13]

The novel as a genre tends toward realism; as Johannes Hoffmeister has remarked, "Der Roman erfordert seinem Wesen nach einen gewissen Realismus, eine gewisse Nähe zu den Gegenständen." [14] This was in fact a prevalent opinion among German critics and theorists in Hölderlin's period. Merck, for example, as well as Blanckenburg, demanded of the German novel objective depiction of contemporary reality.[15] Hölderlin, on the other hand, was aware that by nature he shunned "das Gemeine und

[11] Ronald Peacock, *Hölderlin* (London 1938), p. 94—in general, an admirable book.

[12] Peacock, *op. cit.*, pp. 70 f.

[13] *Marbacher Schillerbuch* (Stuttgart and Berlin, 1905), p. 291. Vischer's attitude in this lecture is annoyingly *spießbürgerlich* and patronizing, but he does make a few sound points.

[14] Johannes Hoffmeister, *Hölderlin und die Philosophie*, 2. Aufl. (Leipzig, 1944), p. 45.

[15] See most recently H. Rudolf Vaget, "Johann Heinrich Merck über den Roman," *PMLA* 83 (1968), pp. 347–356.

Gewöhnliche im wirklichen Leben,[16] whereas under Frau
Gontard's beneficent influence his imagination had been
for a time "williger, die Gestalten der Welt in sich auf-
zunehmen." [17]

In *Hyperion* there is very little realistic detail, and
Gegenstände are not simply things. The milieu, so essential as condition and standard of the hero's progress in the
"novel of development," is only minimally present here;
the inner world is of more moment than the outer. Fixa-
tion in time and place is unimportant; we are more than
halfway through the story before a specific historical event
is referred to and a footnote provides the date of the action
(II, 6). Once, we hear of Hyperion's fishing; it is not, however, for food or sport but to relieve emotional tension (I,
83). Twice, we catch a glimpse of Diotima at her kitchen
stove, but it is a solemn "Feuerheerd" and she a vestal of
the "allwohlthätige Flamme" engaged in a "heilig prie-
sterlich Geschäft" (I, 100; II, 13). A few objects in her
room are mentioned, but as hallowed and in spiritual
league with her (I, 95). So are her flowers and trees; but her
human connections are tenuous. Her mother is a rarefied,
bodiless ideal, her father non-existent, her brother a single
passing reference.

Hyperion's mother is once briefly introduced (I, 31)
and never mentioned again; his father is a faint and con-
tradictory characterization. When, after the breakup of his
friendship with Alabanda, Hyperion returns to his native
island, it is "um meinen Gärten und Feldern zu leben" (I,
65): he appears in possession, and his parents do not figure

---

[16] Letter of November 12, 1798, to Neuffer; StA 6, No. 167, lines 49 f.
"Wirklich" is probably used here in the Swabian sense of "gegenwärtig,"
contemporary.

[17] To Neuffer, February 16, 1797; StA 6, No. 136, lines 18 f.

at all in his last sojourn at home. There is nothing whatever to prepare us for the father's extreme rejection of his son "in this life and the next" because of his patriotic activities (II, 49). We are reminded of the old Graf Moor misguidedly disowning his nobler son.

These personages, and others in *Hyperion,* seem posited for the moment, functions of the hero's soul, projections of a mood or idea, with nothing to suggest their physical appearance, no definite contour or continuity. This is the way of the lyric poet, not the novelist or dramatist. Interconnection and encounter, vital to a play and normally to a novel, are factors much neglected in *Hyperion.* Persons are for the most part brought in singly and in relation to the hero, not one another. This makes for single-thread narration instead of a cross-weave texture. There is, for instance, no trace of a meeting between Hyperion's parents and Adamas or of their reaction to his teaching of and travels with the boy. Alabanda and Diotima never face each other, nor do Notara and Alabanda. The revolutionaries of the Nemesis league appear only briefly and only to Hyperion and Alabanda; they have no connection with the Greek revolt and no social context.

Bellarmin, as we have already noted, is a completely colorless assumption, a name to which the hero can address his reminiscent monologue. In a late letter, Hyperion calls him "du lezter meiner Lieben" (II, 59), but there is nothing to show that he is more than a recent and chance acquaintance of this Greek visitor to Germany. No attempt is made to realize their meeting or their emotional relationship. Hyperion rather awkwardly exempts Bellarmin from his condemnation of the Germans in the penultimate letter without explaining why he does so.

Almost as colorless as Bellarmin is Notara. It is he, we

are left to infer, who is introduced, without name, as "ein Bekannter" and a little later (with no intervening development) greeted tenderly as "mein Freund" (I, 85, 11; 87, 11). Some time thereafter his name is first used (I, 94, 15), but only after a considerable interval is he both named and identified as the friend with whom Hyperion is staying (I, 110, 18 f.). Not until well on in the second volume is he given an attribute: "klug" (II, 12), and this brief letter shows him as a man of affairs. The characterization is piecemeal and faint, and it is significant that a scholar who has made a close study of *Hyperion* could take Notara to be Diotima's father.[18]

Adamas represents the Hamann-Herder creed of *Begeisterung,* a powerful force in Hölderlin's spiritual world. He too is not clearly outlined or localized. As an inspired and inspiring *Wanderlehrer* and all too transient father figure, he doubtless had a personal value for Hölderlin. He wanders into the story from afar and, after kindling in the boy an enthusiasm for Nature and ancient Greece and a sense for Man's inborn divinity ("Es ist ein Gott in uns," I, 27), he wanders out of Hyperion's world again, seeking, like Lessing's Derwisch, a better people in the depths of Asia. Adamas is nowhere objectively described, and we hear no word from his lips until the last moments of farewell. He is a spiritual presence, an intellectual atmosphere, not a person with substance and outline. At the end he assumes mystical grandeur as a kind of Klopstockian God-Father: "er lächelte groß, und seine Stirne breitete vor den

---

[18] L. Ryan, *Hölderlins "Hyperion"* (1965), pp. 185, 198, 209. H. A. Korff, *Geist der Goethezeit,* 2. Aufl. (Leipzig 1949), vol. 3, p. 101, speaks of Diotima's "Eltern" as blessing her betrothal, so he too seems to have taken Notara to be her father.

Sternen des Morgens sich aus und sein Auge durchdrang die Räume des Himmels." [19]

Alabanda is the only person of whose outward appearance we are given a hint. Yet he too is idealized and symbolical, a reincarnated ancient hero, "die alte Heroënnatur" (II, 26) with a Roman cast, "eine Römernatur" (II, 62), a Greek with a "glühenden verbrannten Römerkopfe" (I, 40).[20] But he is also a more modern type of flawed hero, shadowed by association with an eighteenth-century secret society. There is something of the doomed Karl Moor about him in his last phase: "Wie die Mittagssonne vom blaichen Himmel, funkelte sein großes ewiglebendes Auge vom abgeblühten Gesichte mich an" (II, 27). He too is subjectively attached to his author: he personifies Hölderlin's wish for heroism and action, while Hyperion more fully incorporates his elegiac, contemplative disposition. Alabanda is the side of Hölderlin that admonishes him "klage nicht, handle!" (I, 8, 14), Hyperion the side that, Werther-like, sees the illusion in "Aktivität" and, Tasso-like, must sing its "Klage." [21]

[19] I, 26 (fourth letter); cf. *Messias*, 1. Gesang, 139 ff.: "Sprach der ewige Vater, . . ./. . . Ich breite mein Haupt durch die Himmel, / Meinen Arm durch die Unendlichkeit aus."

[20] Hölderlin, like other writers of this time, mingles Greek and Roman mythologies and usually refers to Greek divinities by their Latin names. Diotima invokes "die hohen Spartanischen Frauen" and "die große Römerin" (II, 43, 101) equally as models of heroic dying for a "griechisch Mädchen" (II, 102).

[21] Werther on *Aktivität*: see "den 20. Julius." The problem of action was in the air at this time; cf., e.g., Kleist's friend Brockes, whose maxim was "Handeln ist besser als Wissen" (Kleist's letter to Wilhelmine, January 31, 1801); or Jean Paul's admonition to his son: "Vorzüglich handle! O in Thaten liegen mehr hohe Wahrheiten als in Büchern" (*Sämtl. Wke.*, Berlin 1841, vol. 13, p. 308); and cf. Hölderlin's estimate of his countrymen as "thatenarm und gedankenvoll" (*An die Deutschen*). This is doubt-

There is more of physical passion in the Hyperion-Alabanda relation than in the Hyperion-Diotima one; it reaches terms of bridal ardor (I, 53, 6; 60, 6 f.; II, 41, 12), suggesting a homosexual heightening of the friendship cult which the young Hölderlin's circle had derived from Klopstock and his Göttingen followers. The jealousy, hostility, divorce, and reunion that Hyperion and Alabanda experience together are unmatched in the Hyperion-Diotima connection. This too is consonant with Hölderlin's life, in which male friendships played a greater role than the comparatively brief and spiritual heterosexual attachments.

Alabanda's life, like that of his alter ego, is maimed and frustrated. As a reincarnated antique *heros,* he too should have been born "ein Jahrtausend früher" (I, 7); his lot, like Diotima's, was cast in an alien age. He too has some qualifications to be the hero of the novel. He is the very paragon of manhood: "Wo ist ein Mann, wenn ers nicht war?", yet he can show womanly devotion and tenderness. He seconds Diotima's educative role in teaching his friend to accept life's vicissitude with quiet courage: "wie er, ohne ein Wort, mit seiner großen Ruhe mich lehrte, den freien Lauf der Welt neidlos und männlich zu verstehen!" (II, 62 f.).

If Diotima's belief in immortality rests on her conception of Nature as a loving family (I, 102), Alabanda's, equally characteristic, is based on a conviction of the indestructible vitality of the individual organism. In his last

---

less one reason for the great contemporary effect of Fichte's activism. The admonition quoted in the second letter of *Hyperion,* "klage nicht, handle!", as Emil Petzold long ago surmised (*Hölderlins Brot und Wein,* 1896; 1967 reprint, p. 28), pretty surely echoes a passage in one of Fichte's lectures (*Sämtl. Wke.,* ed. I. H. Fichte (Berlin 1845–46), vol. 6, p. 345).

conversation with Hyperion, Alabanda argues for the absolute autonomy of the individual: he feels in himself a life that no god or man has created, that is "anfanglos" and therefore "endlos" and "unzerstörbar" (II, 90 f.)—a towering Fichteanism. And yet the man who asserts this proud vitalism and sovereignty thereupon lets himself be slaughtered by a secret society he does not believe in, but whose orders he obeys to the letter, refusing even to disclose the place of the "Blutgericht" (II, 89, 17; 92, 10). His final sacrifice of withdrawal from the lives of the lovers proves ironically futile, for Diotima is already dead.

It is a contrived arrangement that makes Alabanda tell his life story to Hyperion twice, each time on his own impulse. The first occasion is early in their acquaintance; the seventh letter reports: "Er erzählte mir nun sein Schiksaal; mir war dabei, als säh' ich einen jungen Herkules mit der Megära im Kampfe" (I, 52). Characteristically, we are given Hyperion's reaction to the story, not the story itself. This is not told us for fifty letters more, near the end of the novel, when Alabanda begins "Laß mich dir erzählen . . ." (II, 83), and goes on for some five pages. Hölderlin's concern at this point is to motivate Alabanda's departure. But the latter's unfaithfulness to the *Bund* and his apprehended unfaithfulness to Hyperion and Diotima are of quite different orders and hardly comparable. His syllogism "Verpflichtung brach ich um des Freundes willen, Freundschaft würd' ich brechen um der Liebe willen," is more neat than sound, and when it culminates in the assertion "Um Diotimas willen würd' ich dich betrügen und am Ende mich und Diotima morden" (II, 87/88), we see how strained the motivation is.

The order of Alabanda's story itself is needlessly confusing. He begins "Ich gieng einst hülflos an dem Hafen von Triest" (II, 83). The next sentence, however, does not go on from there, but for no apparent reason jumps back in time and place: "Das Kaperschiff, worauf ich diente, war einige Jahre zuvor gescheitert"—casting him ashore at Sevilla! It takes another two pages for his account to come around again to the harbor of Triest (II, 85), where it had made a false start.

The groups of persons who appear from time to time in the story lack objective reality and seem invented only to give resonance to a prevailing mood. The "Sonderlinge" who meet in Notara's garden remain undifferentiated (I, 111). Who and how many are in the party that goes to Athens and listens to Hyperion's lecture? "Wir sprachen untereinander. . . . Einer sagte . . . der andere . . . rief einer . . . unterbrach mich einer . . . erwiedert' einer von den Freunden" is the extent of the individuation (I, 138 ff.). For the farewell scene, Notara "und die andern Freunde . . . alle" appear (II, 13), but Diotima's brother, postulated for an earlier context, is omitted.

The emissaries of the "Bund der Nemesis" who appear so suddenly in the vague moonlight (I, 55 ff.) are plainly emotional in origin. Hölderlin speaks of them as "etliche" and as "meist hager und blaß," as though he had in mind a larger number than the three he then introduces as speakers. He tries to individuate these three, but his terms, limited to facial aspect, remain abstract, and their program and procedure ill defined. It is significant that Hölderlin does not finally dispose of them. They stop speaking: "Sie . . . brachen ab" (I, 59)—that is all. They cease to exist when Hyperion leaves the room; it is the psychic effect they release in him that matters to the author.

These are not figures of reality so much as hallucinations induced by severe emotional shock. The hero has just been horrified by the disclosure of a hard, foreign trait in his bosom friend: cold, hostile mockery. Hyperion is "wie aus den Wolken gefallen" (I, 55, 9) and seems to face a stranger. At this instant these sinister forms enter the room, like symbols of alienation, shattering what one may call an ardent romance. Hyperion speaks here in expressly feminine, virtually hysterical terms: "Mir war, wie einer Braut, wenn sie erfährt, daß ihr Geliebter insgeheim mit einer Dirne lebe. O es war der Schmerz nicht, . . . den man am Herzen trägt, wie ein Kind, und in Schlummer singt. . . ." The revulsion is then described with Laocoönian details of invasion and victimization in a "fürchterliche Umarmung" (I, 60).

On a less frantic but still emotional level, this pseudo-mythical trio symbolizes the age-old sense of the precariousness of human happiness: "Je glüklicher du bist, um so weniger kostet es, dich zu Grunde zu richten, und die seeligen Tage, wie Alabanda und ich sie lebten, sind wie eine jähe Felsenspize, wo dein Reisegefährte nur dich anzurühren braucht, um unabsehlich, über die schneidenden Zaken hinab, dich in die dämmernde Tiefe zu stürzen" (I, 50/51).

VII. *Plot, Place, and Time*

If the characters in *Hyperion* show a personal-emotional relevance which we associate with lyrical writing, so do the happenings and places. As in Klopstock's *Messias*—a work notoriously more lyric than epic—feelings and the inward effect of events are made more vivid than the events themselves. The chance meeting of Hyperion and Alabanda (after preliminary circling and gazing) is a case in point. The author resorts to a stock *Raubüberfall* (I, 40 f.) which remains unreal and dreamlike in every respect. Though apparently unarmed, the hero has no difficulty in warding off the unforeseen attack of two sword-brandishing brigands— they were, as the lyrical *Ich* already knows, tired from "other work"—and he quietly resumes his journey. In a moonlit clearing he finds Alabanda, who recognizes his voice, though he has never before heard it, and who tells him of his own earlier brush with the same pair of brigands. A small but revealing detail is Alabanda's odd use of a word: "daß die beiden, auf die ich stieß, wären *fort-*

[72]

geschickt [my italics] worden von ihm" (I, 42, 1 f.). They were not beaten off, but sent off by him; in emotional value and effect, they were *Liebesboten* establishing an ardent friendship. That they were robbers who (we again are left to infer) killed his horse and would have killed him, is unimportant; the dramatic-epic potential of the scene is wholly ignored.

This is not an ordinary encounter of two adventurous young men; it is rather the contrast and harmonizing of two opposite *Seelen,* or the two sides of one. This is expressed by the magnificent picture of the twin mountain torrents, "ergreiffend und ergriffen," [1] and the following antiphonal paragraph (I, 43, 10–44, 12). Here the *vita activa* and the *vita contemplativa* are for a brief, brilliant interval blended and reconciled. And it is again characteristic of the present-time hermit that Alabanda, like Diotima, lives on as a spiritual essence in Nature; a mighty thunderstorm passing overhead, or the play of ocean waves, or eagles circling about high peaks can bring him alive again in the heart of his friend (I, 44/45).

The first meeting of Hyperion and Diotima (thirteenth letter) is suffused with lyric emotion and quite unrealistic. It is prepared for by an elaborate prelude of "Festzeit" mood in the narrator and springtime release in the people, of exquisite Nature pictures on land and sea, of mysterious presentiments of the approach of the divine. But the actual encounter is veiled in reticent adoration: "So lagst du hingegossen, süßes Leben, so bliktest du auf, erhubst dich, standst nun da, in schlanker Fülle, göttlich ruhig, und das himmlische Gesicht noch voll des heitern Entzükens, worinn ich dich störte!" (I, 90). The realist would

---

[1] Cf. Goethe's *Ganymed:* "umfangend umfangen."

ask: what did she look like? what did she rise from? what
was delighting her? was the scene outdoors or indoors? We
are given no more setting than in Hölderlin's poems to
Diotima—where, also, she is typically the serene life, he the
disturber. Only much later, and again in retrospect, do we
get a clue to the location: Hyperion alludes to "den Bogen-
gängen des heiligen Walds" behind Diotima's garden
where he first saw her (I, 127). The words suggest a cathe-
dral, and the scene that now ensues there (I, 127 f.) is on a
religious plane of etherealized love; reality all but vanishes.
The locale is finally confirmed in an otherworldly spirit
when the dying Diotima directs that her ashes be deposited
in the woods at the place where they first met (II, 105).

The setting of their subsequent meetings is not only
unspecific but varies with the author's "pathetic" needs.
Notara's house, where Hyperion stays, is described as high
up on a mountainside (I, 85/86). But when Notara first
takes him to Diotima's house, it is cozily located "nur
einige hundert Schritte von uns am Fuße des Bergs" (I, 94,
17 f.). A few days later, "they" (unspecified) come up for a
return call; Hyperion and Diotima walk together in
Notara's garden and stand "vorn am Rande des Berggip-
fels," from which they can look far off "in den unendlichen
Osten." They are above a steep cliff, a "schrökende Tiefe";
far below stretch extensive dark forests, with rocky ledges
and foaming torrents (I, 97/98). This landscape, which
takes on features of the Swiss Alps, seems unfamiliar to
Diotima, though she lives "around the corner"! It is a
landscape emotionally conceived to set her off as an ethe-
real, all but winged spirit poised over a dread abyss, held
fast as yet by her lover's reverent solicitude.

At one point, Diotima is said to have counted on her
fingers the steps ("Treppen") down from Hyperion's

dwelling to her house (I, 110, 8 f.). This again would indicate a short distance.[2] Yet when Hyperion goes "zu ihr hinab" it seems a much longer way! He looks to clouds and winds for omens of what to expect, "wie es mit mir seyn werde in einer Stunde!" He is glad if he meets with a friendly face and greeting, or a little girl comes out of the woods offering strawberries, or the owner of an orchard he passes invites him to take a handful of cherries (I, 115/116). This is an entirely different stretch! In the earlier passage, Hölderlin was giving a picture of Gretchen-like confiding innocence; in the later one, a lover's gamut of feelings on the emotionally long way to a tryst. Hölderlin's landscape at large and at intimate range is subjective and lyrical. His Greece is almost never pictured realistically or even impressionistically; for all his travel-book borrowings, it remains a landscape of the soul.

Hölderlin's view of the Greeks themselves was colored by his lyric, non-dramatic temper. He saw them through a mood of elegy and longing, not as figures of action and enterprise, of mundane warlike or erotic adventure. They stirred in him a never-ending lament: "Und diese Todtenklage, sie ruht nicht aus" (*Diotima*). When at the beginning of the second Book Hyperion confesses "Ich liebe diß Griechenland überall" (I, 83), we sense that this is a German Philhellene speaking; a native Greek would not put it thus. And when he goes on "Es trägt die Farbe meines Herzens. Wohin man siehet, liegt eine Freude begraben," his colors are fully revealed. Greece is a splendid sepulchre, "wo die Göttersöhne/Schlafen, das trauernde Land der Griechen" (*Der Main*); the glorious dead are the truly living. On the

---

[2] Later on, with her last strength, she manages to go "oft" uphill to the house where Hyperion had lived (II, 98). This too does not suggest a great distance or height.

[75]

day in Athens, Diotima begins to share her lover's feeling that the dead now walk the earth, while those who should live lie buried: "daß jezt die Todten oben über der Erde gehn und die Lebendigen, die Göttermenschen drunten sind" (II, 70). Such a view, needless to say, is the opposite of realistic.

It accords with the inward nature of the work that at crucial moments when in novel or drama we should expect action and agitated speech, Hölderlin has his hero "die" or lapse into a trance.[3] At their first love meeting both Hyperion and Diotima "die" in this fashion: "Es ist hier eine Lüke in meinem Daseyn," Hyperion writes; "ich starb, und wie ich wieder erwachte, lag ich am Herzen des himmlischen Mädchens." After an interval his lost speech returns and he wakes his "stille Begeisterte vollends wieder ins Daseyn" (I, 128). At Diotima's final reappearance in spirit he similarly "blacks out": "mein Denken entschlummerte in mir," and he recovers words "da ich wieder erwacht war" (II, 122).

It is significant that this spiritual reunion takes place on German soil, in a *Feldeinsamkeit* that shows Swabian features. In such passages the Greek costume becomes transparent. Diotima is not really "ein griechisch Mädchen" (II, 102, 5), though she has attained the spiritual rank of the ancient Greeks as Hölderlin saw them; she is a German lover's German soul-mate.

The modern Greeks, on the other hand, are seen as an untutored *Naturvolk* of alternate charm and savagery, a far cry from their illustrious forebears. The picture of camp life in the forty-fifth letter (II, 36 ff.) is naïve and amateurish: the motley "army" of all ages, with women

---

[3] Already the "Untergehen" in the embraces of friendship (I, 61, 6 f.) seems to indicate a swoon.

and children attached; the leader without training who undertakes to train them; the marching about, the council of war with its vague plans, the talk and story-telling by the evening campfires—all this is more idyl than military reality. From a practical point of view, it is unreasonable that Alabanda, the older, more experienced, more martial, is given no share in the drilling or the war councils; Hyperion appears in sole command, and his friend participates only as a companion in relaxation at the end of the day (II, 39).

Nowhere are plot and action of the novel less convincing than in the account of this unpromising "campaign." The sack of Misistra and the final naval battle sound like distant reports rather than present happenings. Here again Alabanda is not shown participating at Hyperion's side, though it had been his dearest wish to fall and be buried with his friend (I, 62, 3 f.); only after the battle does he "hear" of his whereabouts and seek him out. The hero meanwhile, unconscious from a wound, had been carried from the scene by a convenient servant and surgeon an instant before the grappled ships blew up in flames (II, 60 ff.)—the stock device of the last-minute rescue. When a non-novelist undertakes to write a *Roman,* he is apt to fall into *das Romanhafte.*

As a person and as a poet, Hölderlin lived constantly in vivid connection with his past; it was always potentially present and relivable; the backward view was for him an unfailing source of inspiration. In *Hyperion* the hero's feeling again and again "loops back" into the past, a procedure that can confuse the "epic"-minded reader but deepens the rich lyric texture of the work. This is both the consequence and, what is more, the cause of the retrospective-letters technique. As Hyperion relives his story in telling it to Bellarmin, its emotions are renewed, sometimes intensely: "Der Schmerz wird neu, es wiederholt die Klage/Des Lebens labyrinthisch irren Lauf" [or "exzentrische Bahn"]. In a work whose essential life is inner, not outer-factual, whose action is reported, not shown, there can be no hard-and-fast line between emotions experienced and re-experienced. Temporal relations tend to be blurred. We move back and forth in time as mood and memory, not as the chronology of a forthright *historisch* account would dictate. Anticipations and recalls, incursions of the happy past into the mournful present, and the interfusion of experiences in recollection are all characteristic of this prolonged prose elegy.

One example of an emotionally determined tense has already been noted: Diotima's putting her "Wunschtraum" of Hyperion's future career into sustained past indicative instead of "unreal" pluperfect subjunctive (II, 70–72). Another emotional transcending of time limits occurs earlier, in the brief twenty-second letter. There Hyperion writes that in order to be able to speak of the dead Diotima at all he has to persuade himself that she lived ages ago, that her story is hearsay to him. Yet in writing this he slips from the past into the present tense: "Ich muß vergessen, was sie ganz *ist* [italics mine], wenn ich von ihr sprechen soll" (I, 105). For him, she still lives, and to confront her living image is to suffer anew a death of ecstasy and a death of grief. Feeling defies time and tense and the "realities" of life and death.

In the next letter, after foreshadowings in the two preceding ones, the stark finality of Diotima's grave is suddenly introduced (I, 106). This letter and the following one tell of bereavement and despair, all *before* the height of

[78]

happy love is recounted in the twenty-fifth letter. The twenty-sixth then returns to the lonely hermit, but only to contrast with his gloomy present a happy scene from the sunlit past (I, 111 ff.).

A further instance of how timeless emotion complicates the time levels of narration is provided by the ending of the twenty-ninth letter. After recalling from long ago the passionate scene in which Diotima fully avowed her love, Hyperion the letter-writer, overcome by the feelings of that scene, slips from the past tense into the present: "die Sinne vergehn mir und der Geist entflieht" (as though he were on the verge of another "blackout"). Then, as if he were still a participant in that agitated scene, but at the same time his present, narrator self who knows how things ended, or the creative author fashioning his story, he goes on: "Ich seh', ich sehe wie das enden muß," and he concludes with the picture, quoted earlier, of the rudderless ship smashed like an infant against the rocks (I, 136)—a picture, one might add, of unique cruelty among the innumerable references to children in this novel.

One episode in *Hyperion* that betrays an overwhelmingly personal, emotional motivation is the hero's trip to Germany and his consequent condemnation of the Germans. This episode is manifestly "interior," and the author takes no pains to render it outwardly plausible. We gather from the late letters that sometime after Diotima's death Hyperion journeyed to Germany, and it is from there he has evidently returned when the novel opens. In Germany, it seems, he met Bellarmin. But not a word is said of their association there. Bellarmin is given no *Umwelt;* he casts no shadow on his native heath. There is no hint of an exchange about the conditions which the fifty-ninth letter castigates, no allusion to a sharing of the "himmlische Frühling" that brought such an illumination to Hyperion, no thought of his confiding his recent anguish to this "last of his dear ones." The opening of the third letter makes it plain that the story is unknown to Bellarmin and that he had written requesting it. So even here Hyperion remains alone, and the book maintains its character as a lyric soliloquy.

The second letter poses a particular problem with its famous lament

> Ach! wär' ich nie in eure Schulen gegangen. Die Wissenschaft, der ich in den Schacht hinunter folgte, von der ich, jugendlich thöricht, die Bestätigung meiner reinen Freude erwartete, die hat mir alles verdorben.
> Ich bin bei euch so recht vernünftig geworden, habe gründlich mich unterscheiden gelernt von dem, was mich umgiebt, bin nun vereinzelt in der schönen Welt. . . ." (I, 11 f.)

The terms of this lament: going to school, in youthful folly pursuing knowledge down its long shaft, *becoming* rational, *learning* to distinguish oneself from one's environment (Fichte's *Ich* and *Nicht-Ich*?)—all argue an early and prolonged schooling and do not comport with the notion of a mature traveler sojourning briefly in a foreign country. Nor would the later Hyperion, after all his disillusioning experiences, have expected "reine Freude" any more. Why should a Greek of adult years, who has undergone all his major trials and formative fortunes in his native land, be so agitated over a late and minor encounter with German rationalists? The idea is so unlikely that at least one historian of the German novel was led to assume that Hyperion had originally been schooled in Germany and returned there on a later visit.[4] The explanation, of course, is that Hyperion is Hölderlin. Realistically speaking, Germany should mean little to this foreign visitor; emotionally, to the German poet under the thin Greek mask, it means everything.

---

[4] Heinrich Spiero, *Geschichte des deutschen Romans* (Berlin 1950), pp. 45 f. A reviewer of the second (1822) edition of *Hyperion* had likewise concluded "Der junge Grieche hat . . . in Deutschland studirt" (StA 3, p. 329).

VIII. *Vorrede* and *Scheltrede*

Neither the *Vorrede* which introduces the book nor the *Scheltrede* which all but concludes it is of a nature to have won friends for Hölderlin's new novel. They are utterances of increasingly personal implication that bear on the poet's relations to his contemporaries, specifically "die Deutschen," who are only here named but are perceptible at other points under the neo-Greek dress of this story. The *Vorrede* divides them into two classes of readers and declares in advance that neither class will understand the work or receive it with "Liebe." A diffident young author, inwardly all too sure of their unfavorable verdict, over-compensates his diffidence by assuming a disdainful attitude toward the reading public.

One thinks by contrast of the introduction to *Werther*, whose author-editor is sure of his readers' appreciation of his efforts ("weiß, daß ihr mir's danken werdet"—Goethe uses the second person, Hölderlin the third) and appeals unabashedly to their sympathy for his hero, of whose personal reality and pathetic fate one is at once persuaded. Hölderlin, on the other hand, speaks of his story as a "Buch" which could have been written one way or another; the actuality implied by "wo sich das Folgende zutrug" is contradicted by the following lines which admit that the author decided on a Greek setting because it suited the elegiac character of his hero—Hyperion is only now named, whereas warm sympathy thrusts "der arme Werther" into Goethe's very opening line. It was not needful or politic for Hölderlin to tell his readers that he had come to feel ashamed of his excessive solicitude about their opinion ("daß mich das wahrscheinliche Urtheil des Publikums so übertrieben geschmeidig gemacht"). Considering that, after publishing the "*Thalia*-Fragment" several years before, he was now giving them only half a novel and asking them to wait for the rest, the young author was hardly in a position to be impatient with his potential public.[1]

Brief, even abrupt, as it is, the *Vorrede* shows some interesting features of Hölderlin's style. His fondness for the organic parallel is revealed in his speaking of his work as a plant or flower; his musical sense in his apprehending tragic conflicts as dissonances; his basic triadic rhythm in the fact that the criticism of his anticipated readers is stated thrice, in varying terms:

1) . . . die einen werden es lesen, wie ein Compendium, und um das *fabula docet* sich zu sehr bekümmern, indeß die andern gar zu leicht es nehmen, und beede Theile verstehen es nicht.
2) Wer blos an meiner Pflanze riecht, der kennt sie nicht,

[1] It was to be two and one-half years before the second volume appeared, a delay that Hölderlin could not have foreseen and probably was not responsible for. See StA 3, 313 f.

und wer sie pflükt, blos, um daran zu lernen, kennt sie auch nicht.

3) Die Auflösung der Dissonanzen in einem gewissen Karakter ist weder für das bloße Nachdenken, noch für die leere Lust.

The three sentences maintain a similar structure while the factors within them change. Parallelism and antithesis are distinguishing marks of Hölderlin's style.

Moreover, the first two formulations stand in a chiastic arrangement that is another predilection of his, an a b b a order: those who take it as moral teaching/those who take it as light entertainment//those who merely sniff the fragrance/those who dissect the flower. The third formulation then, returning to the order of the first, has a balancing, summarizing weight, bringing in as it does the deeper theme of the novel, the resolution of dissonances in the character of the hero and in life. It is in small compass that Hölderlin's careful composition is most evident.

A minor peculiarity of his style is illustrated by the position of *sich* and the second *es* in formulation (1): the retarding of personal pronouns. Similarly, in the opening letter, we read "schrökt ja aus meinen Träumen mich auf" (I, 8); in the seventh, "und wies sein todtes Roß mir" (I, 42). Sometimes a subject noun is thus held back: "Wie ein zärtlichscheidender, fühlte zum leztenmale sich in allen seinen Sinnen mein Geist" (II, 60); the similarly balanced close of the sixth letter (I, 38) has already been cited (Chapter II). A verb too may thus be held in suspense, as in the final letter: "wenn ich hinauf, wo wild die Rose um den Steinpfad wuchs, den warmen Hügel gieng" (II, 119). Sometimes, but not always, considerations of rhythm and euphony seem to determine the order, as in the climactic finale of Diotima's vision: "und zu Thaten geleitete, schöner als Kriegsmusik, die jungen Helden Helios Licht" (II, 72).[2]

The most acute instance of personal-emotional relevance in the whole book is the formidable invective or *Scheltrede* which fills its next-to-last letter. None of those who have extolled the perfect novel structure of *Hyperion* has ever demonstrated the structural necessity of this letter. It makes no helpful contribution to plot and character. In the economy of the novel it can only be called a divagation, an excrescence, a blemish; one can try to explain it, but it cannot be justified on artistic grounds.

Comparable criticism can be found in other writers of that idealistic, humane age, but—this is the decisive difference—not so sharp and specific and not injected at such length into a poetic work. Several years earlier, in the sixth of the letters *Über die ästhetische Erziehung des Menschen*, Schiller had recognized the plight of modern, fractionalized Man, who has ceased to represent whole, harmonious humanity and become a mere "Abdruck seines Geschäfts, seiner Wissenschaft."[3] But Schiller is expressly speaking of "die neuere Menschheit" and in the dispassionate tone of the social philosopher.

Several years later, in *Der Archipelagus* (lines 241 ff.), Hölderlin gives us a glimpse of benighted, godless contemporary Man: "Aber weh! es wandelt in Nacht, es

---

[2] Hölderlin uses such retardation with artistic effect in poems, e.g., *Der Zeitgeist*, where in the opening lines, "Zu lang schon waltest über dem Haupte mir / Du in der dunkeln Wolke, du Gott der Zeit!", extraordinary emphasis, suspense, and mystery are achieved by the withholding of the subject and its identification. This is another feature, it might be added, that Hölderlin shares with Klopstock.

[3] *Schillers sämtliche Werke*, Säkular-Ausg., vol. 12, p. 19.

wohnt, wie im Orkus/ Ohne Göttliches unser Geschlecht,"
chained to incessant production, each one hearing only his
own din in the uproar of the vast workshop. But there, like
Schiller, the poet speaks generally, not aspersing the
Germans by name; he speaks in lament, not accusation,
with compassion for "die Mühe der Armen"; and with his
normal hopefulness he then foresees the dawn of a better
day.[4]

Elsewhere in the novel we hear Hyperion disparaging
his degenerate fellow-men (e.g., I, 35 f., 68 f.); and cer-
tainly his soldiers at Misistra did not measure up to their
illustrious ancestors. But the criticism applies to Greeks.
At the end of the first Book of volume one, the hero, in a
nihilistic mood ("nichts" runs as a somber refrain through
the letter), pours out his scorn upon his fellows, who for
all their pretensions are slaves to fear and darkness and
death (I, 78–80). But this is again very general, and is dis-
counted in the last line: "Wie das alles in mich kam,
begreif ich noch nicht."

The criticism comes nearer home in Hyperion's lecture
at Athens, when he deprecates the domination of reason
and discipline over the Spartans, who consequently re-
mained forever "fragments," not full *Menschen* like the
Athenians. Overdeveloped intellect and reason are declared
to be "die Könige des Nordens" and devoid of "Geistes-
schönheit" (I, 147/148). Here Hölderlin, one feels, is
censuring not merely the Spartans but the still more
"northern" Germans, and perhaps voicing his resentment

---

[4] A generation later, Emerson, in his Phi Beta Kappa oration, "The
American Scholar" (1837), likewise saw modern Man "subdivided and
peddled out, . . . a good finger, a neck, a stomach, an elbow, but never
a man," etc.

at the inroads of *Zucht* and *Verstand* in his own life and work. But if this passage may be thought to presage the later tirade in a general way, it is still very far from the unveiled and unsparing attack on the Germans as a nation that makes the fifty-ninth letter unique among Hölderlin's writings.

Had he not specifically named the Germans in this indictment, it might have stood, like Schiller's, as an indictment of contemporary civilization. But where Schiller, from the more intellectual angle of *Humanität,* saw a failure to fulfill the idea of the "complete man," Hölderlin, with his stronger *Natursinn,* saw a betrayal of Nature. Modern Man, alias the German, is condemned for his impious unnaturalness ("gottverlaßne Unnatur," II, 113, 18), his contempt for Nature, his disregard of her patient benefactions, his ruthless despoliation of her: "Ihr entwürdiget, ihr zerreißt, wo sie euch duldet, die geduldige Natur." But Man is unable to disturb the cycle of her seasons or contaminate her aether (today, we are not so sure of this): "O göttlich muß sie seyn, weil ihr zerstören dürft, und dennoch sie nicht altert und troz euch schön das Schöne bleibt!" (II, 116).

From this disregard for Nature, the fundamental Beauty, follows the disregard for poets and artists, for genius as the highest form of Nature; "die göttliche Natur und ihre Künstler" are one (II, 118). A people who have lost the sense for Nature and Beauty have lost the sense for genius (II, 118, 1 f.); they spread a blight, "weil sie die Wurzel des Gedeihns, die göttliche Natur, nicht achten, . . . weil sie den Genius verschmähn" (II, 117, 10 ff.). Without love of Nature/Beauty, without respect for genius, there can be no spiritual community such as Hölderlin yearned

[87]

for, no "allgemeiner Geist" as a new "Lebensluft" (II, 118, 2 f.), no *Begeisterung* (which means both inspiration and enthusiasm).

In consequence, men ("die Menschen, die doch alle schöngeboren sind," II, 118, 9) have cast away their birthright; they develop a servile mentality; they are intoxicated with power, yet insecure; in the midst of luxury they feel hunger and worry about their food supply, and their abundant production becomes a curse; they have lost their gods: "der Knechtsinn wächst, mit ihm der grobe Muth, der Rausch wächst mit den Sorgen, und mit der Üppigkeit der Hunger und die Nahrungsangst; zum Fluche wird der Seegen jedes Jahrs und alle Götter fliehn" (II, 118, 9–13). This letter is not simply an arraignment of the Germans of the 1790's; it is a prophetic vision of twentieth-century Man, alienated from Nature, self-impoverished on his exploited Earth.

On its face, however, the letter presents an unmotivated and embarrassing attack on the author's own people, and Hölderlin scholarship has been at some pains to explain and exonerate. Writers have quoted Hölderlin's almost contemporaneous epigram *Der zürnende Dichter* to prove that this wrath is only the negative aspect of love of country.[5] And other poems have been pointed to as balancing and outweighing the present condemnation: *Gesang des Deutschen, An die Deutschen* (the longer form), *Germanien,* and *Deutscher Gesang.* The somewhat earlier letter to Ebel has been cited as testimony to Hölderlin's

---

[5] Already Achim von Arnim, 1828: "dieser Zorn . . . ist eben ein heller Widerschein seiner glühenden Liebe" (StA 3, 319). This is like what Otto Ludwig in *Die Makkabäer* has Lea say of Judah: "Haßt er das Volk, so haßt ers / Aus Liebe. Diesen Haß und diese Liebe / Laß für ihn bürgen" (*Schriften,* ed. Stern and Schmidt, vol. 3, p. 316).

belief in Germany's mission and her contribution to the great intellectual revolution of the future.[6] That letter, however, was not publicly known, and none of the poems just mentioned was published during Hölderlin's lifetime. It is all the more astounding, and a sign of the tolerant, non-nationalistic spirit of late-eighteenth-century Germany, that this slashing attack on the Germans passed without counter-attack. Cotta apparently raised no objection to a feature that would hardly promote the popularity of the book he published. Nor, as far as we know, did Susette, who exerted some influence on its final stage,[7] take exception to this letter. Perhaps she was as much inflamed as Diotima was by her lover's indignation. The anonymous Tübingen reviewer, to be sure, was plainly offended by this "one-sided, harsh, and unjust verdict upon our Germany," but, with mild remonstrance, he charged it to a young Philhellene's over-idealization of ancient Greece. On the basis of soberer knowledge he doubted that "dies wunderbare Geniusland," even in its most brilliant era, ever equaled the picture painted by such German dreamers (StA 3, 325).[8]

A century and more thereafter, a less sparing critic, the young Franz Zinkernagel, in his monograph on the genesis of *Hyperion*, said of this invective: "Wie ein roter Lappen auf einem Trauerkleid nimmt diese Anklage mitten im Berichte seiner Leiden sich aus." [9] For the literary critic,

[6] Letter of January 10, 1797; StA 6, No. 132, lines 45–57.

[7] The "Scheltrede" is not contained in the preliminary versions of *Hyperion*.

[8] Hölderlin's friend Emerich, in a reported letter to him of March 4, 1800, declared himself "entzückt" over the second volume but "empört" over the condemnation of the Germans. See StA 3, 318.

[9] Franz Zinkernagel, *Die Entstehungsgeschichte von Hölderlins "Hyperion"* (Strassburg, 1907), p. 198.

this so drastically expressed opinion touches on the essential point of the matter: the artistic indefensibility of this sudden outburst, the inappropriateness of injecting it at this place in the hero's development and the novel's structure. It throws the foreign costume and the letter fiction to the winds. What would this Greek be seeking in Germany: "Ich foderte nicht viel. . . . Ich suchte unter diesem Volke nichts mehr" (II, 112, 119)? Why should he be telling a German about conditions in Germany? [10] Only at the very end of the letter does he seem to remember that Bellarmin is a German; then he claims to have spoken in Bellarmin's name too and "für alle, die in diesem Lande sind und leiden, wie ich dort gelitten." He does not coldly scoff; he suffers. His anguished plaint continues, in heightened terms, into the following, final letter: "ich war genug gekränkt, von unerbittlichen Belaidigungen, wollte nicht, daß meine Seele vollends sich verblute" (II, 119). Why should a visiting foreigner suffer such agony of soul? And what would be the point in assuring the recipient of a private letter that it speaks out for him and other Germans? Clearly it is meant as a public, printed manifesto.

This letter makes little or no sense in its fictional context. It does make sense as the despairing outcry of Hölderlin over the failure of his countrymen, whom he loves, to come up to his ideal of them; over his consequent failure, feared even now, to find an intellectual home among them. It is his personal emotion that in the middle of the tirade (II, 115, 14–116, 12) alters the construction from third-person statement to direct second-person reproach. He is

[10] Contrariwise, it is Hölderlin speaking to a fellow German about intellectual conditions in Germany when Hyperion remarks "Du weist ja, wie so manche edle Kraft bei uns zu Grunde geht, weil sie nicht genüzt wird" (I, 18)—how should Bellarmin know about wasted talent in Greece?

the blind Oedipus at the gates, the homeless wanderer longing for a community of "schöne Seelen" who honor Nature
and its gods and geniuses, who will receive him and his
work (II, 112, 7 ff.). Farther on in this same letter, Hölderlin identifies himself, as a German poet, with another royal
beggar of antiquity: Ulysses, the despised stranger in his
own house (II, 116, 12 ff.).

To his friend Neuffer, already in June 1798, Hölderlin complains that so few Germans still believe in him, and
he fears that "die harten Urtheile der Menschen" will
finally hound him out of Germany, "at least." [11] In a letter
of the same month to Schiller he speaks of being "von
mancher Seite niedergedrükt." [12] It may be that the indif-
ferent reception of the first volume of *Hyperion* added to
his despondency over his future as a writer in his homeland; the misgivings of his *Vorrede* must then have seemed
prophetic of the public mentality that the *Scheltrede* ar-
raigns. It may be, on the other hand, that some early onset
of mental disturbance had terrified him with a sense of his
destructibleness,[13] a fear that his time was short, that he
might go "klanglos zum Orkus hinab." Such things could
explain a frantic outburst even of a loving, patient, and
modest writer against the stolid unresponsiveness of his
contemporaries. And this time Hölderlin did not, as in the
case of Empedocles' curse upon his countrymen, draw a
deletion line and rescind his condemnation in a reaction

---

[11] StA 6, No. 158, lines 15–18. A few years later, grieving at the prospect of leaving Germany, he puts his plight into the simple, moving words
"was hab' ich lieberes auf der Welt [als mein Vaterland]? Aber sie können
mich nicht brauchen" (to Böhlendorff, December 4, 1801; StA 6, No. 236,
lines 85 f.).

[12] StA 6, No. 159, line 5.

[13] He was aware, as his letters reveal, "daß ich so zerstörbar bin" (to
his mother, January 1799; StA 6, No. 173, line 20).

of forgiving love.[14] The hard sentence was allowed to stand.

It is clear, however, that the Germans are thus singled out for censure because they are *his* people, his hope, his natural audience, not because they are the worst of all nations. And they could have pleaded in their own defense that it is a mark of Germany's cultural eminence in that golden age to have produced a genius capable of judging his fellow-countrymen from so lofty a station. For the *Mustervolk* against which they are here measured never existed save in the mind of a German idealist.

[14] See StA 4, 481, 17 ff.

IX. *Music*

The lyrical nature of *Hyperion* is evidenced by its intimate connection with music. From beginning to end, from the *Vorrede* to the closing lines, the references to music, the similes and metaphors from the realm of music, the perceptions in terms of music, are almost too many to count. Music is a pervasive atmosphere throughout. "Die Auflösung der Dissonanzen in einem gewissen Karakter" is stated at the start as the aim of the work; like the recapitulated theme in a musical composition it comes in again at the close, enriched by the intervening development and enlarged to include "die Dissonanzen der Welt" (I, 3; II, 124).

This novel is a unique creation that stands in the broad border zone between poetry and music. Wilhelm Dilthey long ago recognized its "musical style" that links it with Nietzsche's *Zarathustra*.[1] Marie Crayssac, in her

[1] Wilhelm Dilthey, *Das Erlebnis und die Dichtung*, 8. Aufl. (Leipzig, 1922), p. 414.

Études sur l' "Hyperion," somewhat fancifully declared the reality of its characters to be "that of musical themes which detach themselves from an infinite melody, separate, re-unite, and vanish in a murmur." [2] And Johannes Klein has similarly interpreted *Hyperion* as a texture of motifs that clash, blend, separate, and re-unite, of "Seelenvorgänge" which the narrator could not make visible, but which become credible in the musician Hölderlin's composition.[3]

The free movement back and forth in time, which we earlier noted as significant of the lyrical-emotional temper of *Hyperion,* is not unrelated to certain aspects of musical composition. Anticipation and recall, the preluding of a melody to be developed later and re-echoed still later, the bringing in of a theme from some other level of time or experience to contrast with the present one—all these procedures are as natural to Hölderlin's lyrical sensibility as they are to music. For example, early in the story, in the sixth letter, even before the Hyperion-Alabanda chapter opens, Diotima is introduced, as yet without name, and Hyperion's prophetic soul is likened to a lily swaying in the atmosphere of delightful dreams of her (I, 38)—a finale that seems a Romantic blend of the musical and the pictorial, *Stimmung* and *Bild.* At the same time—such is the transparency of time levels in *Hyperion*—even as he describes this premonition, the hero looks back on the emergence of Diotima as a distant memory. A note of mysterious happy expectancy is struck on his boat trip to Kalaurea,

[2] Marie Crayssac, *Études sur l' "Hyperion" d'Hölderlin* (Nancy, 1924), p. 183.

[3] Johannes Klein, "Die musikalischen Leitmotive in Hölderlins *Hyperion,*" *GRM* 23 (1935), pp. 177–192; reprinted in condensed form in Klein's *Hölderlin in unserer Zeit* (Köln, 1947).

many pages later (I, 86 f.), and then, at the close of the fourteenth letter, Diotima's name is first heard, without further explanation (I, 94); but she is spoken of in the past tense, and it is clear that she is lost. After another interval, her grave is suddenly mentioned, with emphatic iteration (I, 106), even before the love story has been unfolded. Hölderlin as it were moves up the black shadow of death behind life's brightest scenes, as if thereby to enhance their incomparable luster.

At the very zenith of the early Hyperion-Alabanda friendship, the author preludes its end in a striking figure (I, 50/51). It is in keeping with Hölderlin's love of chromatic contrast that, once this ideal friendship is wrecked, its most glowing colors are displayed in a rehearsal of the irrecoverable past (I, 61 f.). Long before Alabanda is finally gone, his life is summed up in an epitaph that with its imagery and melody makes one of the noblest letter closings of the book (II, 62/63).

At the beginning of the second volume, the rushing brook, image of the transiency of all things, presages to the lovers the inevitable passing of their happiness: "So sollt' auch unsre eigne Seeligkeit dahingehn, und wir sahen's voraus" (II, 5). Here again we hear the preluding of the tragic melody to come. Conversely, the motif of the *Geländer* over the abyss, which connotes for the lovers an early thrilling contact (I, 97/98), comes in again in Diotima's farewell, wistfully elaborated in a somber key under the shadow of death (II, 98).

When Hyperion writes to Diotima of the bated fury of the mountain people under his command, he sounds a premonitory note: "Fürchte nichts! Sie werden so wild nicht seyn" (II, 23). This is many pages before he must report a "gewitterhafte Luft" in camp and misgivings about his men (II, 44) and, later still, the savage excesses that bring down the whole enterprise in a crashing collapse.

The persons in *Hyperion* are not realistically rounded figures but rather symbols momentarily illuminated by feeling. Hence they can live and move freely in the bodiless realm of music. They are spiritual essences, *Wesen,* much more than physical bodies. When Diotima for the first time comes so close to Hyperion that her breath touches him, it is not his cheek or hair that feels it but his listening soul: "daß ihr unschuldiger Othem mein lauschend Wesen berührte!" (I, 95).[4] Hyperion says of his inspiring teacher Adamas "wiederholten sich nicht die Melodien seines Wesens in mir?" (1, 20). A radiant evocation of ancient Greece and its inspired youth culminates in musical expression: "In den Hainen, in den Tempeln erwachten und tönten in einander ihre Seelen, und treu bewahrte jeder die entzükenden Accorde" (I, 23).

Alabanda, on hearing Hyperion utter convictions like his own, exclaims "Das ist endlich einmal meine Melodie" (I, 48). Their friendship in its happiest stage is characterized by Hyperion in musical terms: "Nur in den ewigen Grundtönen seines Wesens lebte jeder, und schmuklos schritten wir fort von einer großen Harmonie zur andern" (I, 50). In dejection after the breakup of this comradeship the hero contemplates his fellow-men and finds "überall . . . Mislaut, nur in kindlicher einfältiger Beschränkung fand ich noch die reinen Melodien" (I, 65).

Hölderlin's idea of "ewige Wiederkehr" is deeply connected with his consciousness of musical laws. Hyperion,

---

[4] Similarly, Werther, at his first meeting with Lotte, says not merely "mein Auge" but "meine ganze Seele ruhte auf der Gestalt" (am 16. Junius).

after speaking of Harmodius and Aristogiton, voices his hope that such great characters will needs appear again in the world's history, "daß solche große Töne und größere einst wiederkehren müssen in der Symphonie des Weltlaufs" (I, 112). To the lovers in their new-found bliss it seems as though the old world had died and a new one were beginning with them, "und wir und alle Wesen schwebten, seelig vereint, wie ein Chor von tausend unzertrennlichen Tönen, durch den unendlichen Aether" (I, 132). Not only is the individual being again equated with a musical note, but a whole multitude of coherent harmonious tones forms as it were a new solar system voyaging through endless space—a sublime conception akin to that of the cosmic cloud of melody in *Der Mutter Erde*: "und voll, wie aus Meeren schwingt/Unendlich sich in die Lüfte die Wolke des Wohllauts."

In her valedictory, Diotima conceives of the life of individuals and the universe as melody and harmony in a grand design: "in wandelnde Melodien theilen wir die großen Akkorde der Freude. . . . Wir sind wie die Jungfrauen und die Jünglinge, die mit Tanz und Gesang, in wechselnden Gestalten und Tönen den majestätischen Zug geleiten" (II, 103 f.). And long after her death, her lover reaffirms her faith in like language: "Lebendige Töne sind wir, stimmen zusammen in deinem Wohllaut, Natur!" (II, 123).

In *Hyperion*, the art of words seems constantly to be reaching for the immediacy and immateriality of the art of tones. We are reminded of Walter Pater's dictum "all art constantly aspires towards the condition of music." [5] The language of this novel is often of an exquisite euphony, and yet speech is regarded, in the Romantic spirit, as a

[5] Walter Pater, *The Renaissance*, 5th ed. (London, 1925), p. 135.

medium inferior to music.[6] "Wir sprachen wenig zusammen," says Hyperion; "Man schämt sich seiner Sprache. Zum Tone möchte man werden und sich vereinen in Einen Himmelsgesang" (I, 95). Of another supreme moment, he declares: "Worte sind hier umsonst. . . . Das Einzige, was eine solche Freude auszudrüken vermochte, war Diotima's Gesang, wenn er, in goldner Mitte, zwischen Höhe und Tiefe schwebte" (I, 121). Diotima, "die liebende Schweigende," is loth to speak. It is consistent with the high valuation of music in *Hyperion* that its noblest character finds deepest and fullest expression in singing. The seventeenth letter, one of the most poignant and beautiful in the book, beginning and ending with "ihr(en) Gesang," tries to convey in words the power of this higher language and the quality of a life which, like her song, was "heilig" and "schön" (I, 99).

Existence is equated with music. The life of the world and the inner life of the hero are both characterized in musical terms when he describes himself as "lächerlich begleitet vom Schellenklange der Welt in meines Herzens liebsten Melodien" (I, 44). In a melodious passage he senses the coming of the dawn as music, blending his favorite light and sound motifs in a Romantic synaesthesia: "wenn über mir die Melodie des Morgenlichts mit leisem Laute begann" (I, 30). In like manner, the coming of spring is heralded by aerial melodies: "Wie fernher in schweigender Luft, wenn alles schläft, das Saitenspiel der Geliebten, so umtönten seine leisen Melodien mir die Brust" (I, 74).

[6] See the chapter "Words and Music" in my *Early German Romanticism* (Cambridge, 1929), pp. 194 ff. The brief Hölderlin section of that book (pp. 106–118) points out some respects in which Hölderlin was related to his contemporaries.

In the exalted mood, a *Festzeit* of the soul, in which Hyperion begins the account of his happiest past, it seems like music rising within him: "Wie Jupiters Adler dem Gesange der Musen, lausch' ich dem wunderbaren unendlichen Wohllaut in mir" (I, 85). Before he knew Diotima, he tells us, he was a broken lyre, "ein zerrissen Saitenspiel," that gave forth only few and dying notes (I, 92). His life with her is measured in music: "war sie nicht mein? vereint mit mir in allen Tönen des Lebens?" (I, 108). He will bear life, he tells her, as long as she still lives, "so lange noch Eine Melodie mir tönt"; beyond that lies the soundless desolation of death, "die Todtenstille der Wildniß unter den Sternen" (I, 120).

Memories become music: "denkst du unsrer goldenen Tage nicht mehr?" he asks her, "der holdseeligen, göttlichmelodischen? säuseln sie nicht aus allen Hainen von Kalaurea dich an?" (II, 78). As the hermit surveys his receding past, it becomes for him music, played by a Master according to a mysterious score: "meine Vergangenheit lautet mir oft, wie ein Saitenspiel, wo der Meister alle Töne durchläuft, und Streit und Einklang mit verborgener Ordnung untereinanderwirft" (I, 84).

In one of the most profound passages of the book, the very life of the universe is conceived as music, a heavenly song to which our ears are opened only in the dark of deep suffering: "daß, wie Nachtigallgesang im Dunkeln, göttlich erst in tiefem Laid das Lebenslied der Welt uns tönt" (II, 119). Immortality is music; ultimately the bond between the lovers, living and dead, is that of "lebendige Töne" united in Nature's "Wohllaut"; as that can never be sundered, so they are forever one and inseparable (II, 123).

X. *Latent Meter*

If *Hyperion* is on the borderline between poetry and music, it is also on the borderline between prose and verse. Much of it, one feels, could scarcely be more rhythmical and melodious and still remain prose. In fact, the line is crossed: a great deal of *Hyperion* falls into verse units and familiar meters. Every rereading of this text discloses new ones to the inward ear—not simply pieces that can be artificially excised and made to scan, but such as naturally form sentence, clause, or phrase entities. Needless to say, it is not a matter of intentional "heightening" of prose by verse embellishment, as in the spurious art of many an inferior writer; it is the lyric poet's inborn propensity toward *gebundene Rede* that instinctively tends to cast Hölderlin's thought in such verse molds. His language rhythm is difficult to define; [1] but one factor in its complex undula-

[1] The most elaborate treatment of the subject, *Hölderlins Sprachrhythmus*, by Dietrich Seckel (Leipzig, 1937), 350 pages, is burdened by abstraction and construction.

tions that deserves to be noted is the recurrence of these definite metric waves.

Hölderlin shows a certain fondness for the dactylic hexameter, which ends with the Adonic cadence (′ xx ′ x) that is his favorite close for sentences and paragraphs. Thus the twelfth letter concludes, after a sequence of triadic measures, with the hexameter "wallt der schüchterne Mond am hellen Tage vorüber" (I, 84). Farther on, a long paragraph ends "bis auch mich . . .] in den Schoos der Natur die Wooge der Liebe zurükbringt" (I, 135, 3); two shorter paragraphs end "die Natur . . . nur] Ein begeistertes Echo des Herrlichen, dem sie gehörte" (I, 151, 4 f.), and "aber es ist doch Schade um all' die Größe und Schönheit" (I, 154, 1 f.). Four such hexameters, with brief interruptions, occur in close proximity in Diotima's dream of Hyperion's career:

Ach! nun verließen so leicht sich nicht die geselligen
                                         Menschen;
wie der] Sand im Sturme der Wildniß irrten sie
                         untereinander [nicht mehr, noch
höhnte sich Jugend und Alter, noch fehlt' ein Gastfreund
                                      dem Fremden. . . .
Götter erheiterten wieder [die] verwelkliche Seele der
                                         Menschen.
                                      (II, 71, 8–15)

At the very end, in Hyperion's apostrophe to the eternal beauty of the world, we again hear the roll of hexameters:

du bist; was ist denn der Tod und alles Wehe der
                                      Menschen? . . .
Geschiehet doch alles aus Lust, und endet doch alles mit
                         Frieden. (II, 124)

[101]

Sometimes a hexameter is joined to a pentameter:

> da weht' es oft so bittend und so schmeichelnd,
> oft, wie ein Göttergebot, von den zarten blühenden Lippen.
>
> (I, 99, 6 f.)

Pentameter units are much more frequent.[2] Hölderlin's rhythmical sense and form of thought evidently found a satisfaction in the five-stress measure. Sometimes it constitutes an independent sentence, at other times a subordinate clause, an exclamation, or a modifying phrase of some kind. From the second volume alone one can readily cull almost a score of examples of complete iambic pentameter sentences:

> Das beste ist, du gehst, denn es ist größer.
>
> (II, 10, 18)
>
> Sie sollten nun mein Scheiden auch mir seegnen.
>
> (II, 13, 16)
>
> Ich weiß von nichts mehr, wenn ich sie nicht weiß.
>
> (II, 16, 5)
>
> Sie sind das liebste, was ich dir vertraue.
>
> (II, 21, 8 f.)
>
> Beim Himmel! ich bin überreif zur Arbeit.
>
> (II, 24, 13 f.)
>
> Das war nicht stolz gesprochen, Alabanda.
>
> (II, 26, 8 f.)
>
> Ich bin für dich nichts mehr, du holdes Wesen!
>
> (II, 49, 1)
>
> Den kann ich ohne Schaden mir behalten.
>
> (II, 50, 10)

---

[2] One of the preliminary versions of *Hyperion* was an experiment in iambic pentameter. But this fragmentary "metrische Fassung" (StA 3, pp. 186–198) is prosy and plodding, and there is no echo of its lines in the examples quoted in our chapter.

Er ist so sanft geworden und so still.
                    (II, 50 11 f.)
Nun schreib' ich wieder dir, mein Bellarmin!
                    (II, 59, 3)
Doch hat sie wohl den lezten Brief noch nicht.
                    (II, 66, 2 f.)
Ich hab' es bis aufs Äußerste getrieben.
                    (II, 74, 13)
Auch er war heiter; nur in andrem Sinne.
                    (II, 79, 14 f.)
Das Stillesizen hat dich scheu gemacht.—
                    (II, 81, 11)
Du blikst mich an, als kenntest du mich nicht?
                    (11, 81/82)
Tröste mich nicht, denn hier ist nichts zu trösten,
                (II, 82, 4, with initial trochee)
Ich zog das Götterrecht des Herzens vor.
                    (II, 87, 11)
Was können sie mir nehmen, als mein Blut?
                    (II, 88, 8)
Auch treibt michs immer, mancherlei zu sagen.
                    (II, 101, 4)

Pentameters occur not only singly but in pairs that may together make a complete sentence:

Das gab auch mir ein schmerzliches Verstummen,
worein ich selbst mich nicht zu finden wußte.
                    (I, 134, 3–5)
Da legen wir die Sklavenkleider ab,
worauf das Schiksaal uns sein Wappen gedrükt—
                (II, 29, 6 f., with anapaest)
Ein tiefes Lebensgefühl durchdrang mich noch.
Es war mir warm und wohl in allen Gliedern.
                (II, 60, 1 f., with anapaest)

[103]

Noch wirst du glüklich seyn, rief Alabanda;
Noch ist die schönste Lebenszeit dir übrig.
(II, 66, 12 f.)
Ich zog mich aus und ruht im Sonnenschein
und troknete die Kleider an den Sträuchen.
(II, 84, 3 f.)

In another case, only a "said he" separates the two adjacent pentameters: "Ich darf den Ort nicht nennen, liebes Herz! erwiedert' er; wir sehn vieleicht uns dennoch einmal wieder" (II, 92, 10 f.).

In all these examples there is an almost unvaried iambic beat and a rather matter-of-fact content. But Hölderlin may lighten the movement by introducing one or more anapaests, as he does at times in *Empedokles,* and such "lines" often express livelier emotion too (again only complete sentences are chosen):

O Mädchen! stille zu stehn, ist schlimmer, wie alles.
(II, 44, 9)
Wir sagen uns nichts; was sollten wir uns sagen?
(II, 50, 13)
Wir waren so dem Hafen näher gekommen.
(II, 93, 1)
Du wirsts vollenden in dir, und dann erst ruhn.
(II, 102, 4)
Ich werde seyn; ich frage nicht, was ich werde.
(II, 103, 7)
Zu mächtig war mir meine Seele durch dich,
sie wäre durch dich auch wieder stille geworden.
(II, 100, 8 f.)
O könnt' ich dich sehn in deiner künftigen Schöne!
(II, 104, 14).

The anapaests may actually outnumber the iambs in such a sequence: "wir ringen mit sterblichen Kräften Schönes zu baun" (II, 64, 3). It is interesting that a sense of the meter seems to encourage the use of contracted forms like "sehn," "ruhn," and "baun."

Sometimes it is a trochaic-dactylic pentameter that forms a sentence: "Traure nicht, holdes Wesen, traure nicht!" (II, 30, 16). Or two such trochaic pentameters with initial dactyls may form a main clause: "würd' ich auch da sogar dir nachempfinden,/würde mir Mühe geben, dich zu hassen" (II, 42, 16 f.). The concentration of dactyls can be quite heavy, as in "solch eine Römernatur hab' ich nimmer gefunden" (II, 62, 18).

Not only self-contained whole sentences but any number of other syntactical entities in the text of *Hyperion* fall into this five-stress pattern. There are many principal clauses that form parts of longer sentences:

Die reinen Quellen fodr' ich auf zu Zeugen
(I, 108, 3)
verlaidet ist mir meine eigne Seele
(II, 109, 8 f.)
nun hatt' ich es, das reizende Bekenntniß
(I, 135, 1)
Sie soll uns seegnen, diese theure Mutter
(II, 16, 15 f.)
Er sei das Zeichen zwischen mir und dir
(II, 19, 15)
von dir verbannt mich meine eigene Schaam
(II, 47, 13 f.)
es bleibt uns überall noch eine Freude
(II, 49/50)
entscheide nun mein Schiksaal, theures Mädchen
(II, 77, 10 f.)
Ich glaube, daß wir durch uns selber sind
(II, 90, 13)
Dein Mädchen ist verwelkt, seitdem du fort bist,
ein Feuer in mir hat mälig mich verzehrt
(II, 96, 11 f.)

Such a list could be greatly extended. In addition, there are infinitive phrases of the type "das gute Volk aus seiner Schmach zu ziehn" (II, 32, 11) or "um sich und mir den Abschied abzukürzen" (II, 93, 11). A compound object may take this form: "den Geist von allen Geistern beßrer Zeit,/ die Kraft von allen Kräften der Heroën" (II, 119, 8–10). Subordinate clauses of all kinds, adverbial and adjectival, fall into this pentameter rhythm:

> wenn uns ein großes Ziel vor Augen steht
> (II, 12, 14 f).
> worinn ich mein Beginnen ihm geschrieben
> (II, 49, 18)
> von wo ein sicher Schiff uns weiter bringt
> (II, 76, 3)
> als wär ein zeitverkürzend Spiel verloren
> (II, 80, 1)
> damit er nichts von mir dir schreiben sollte
> (II, 98, 7)
> die Götterfreiheit, die der Tod uns giebt
> (II, 102, 11)

The similes that are so plentiful in *Hyperion* are often cast in this mold. Diotima sees a new Hyperion come forth "wie ein Kristallquell aus der düstern Grotte" (I, 129, 12 f.). The commander likens his mountaineers, grimly biding their time, to an ominous thundercloud "die nur des Sturmwinds wartet, der sie treibt" (II, 23, 12 f.). The lovers' conversations glide away like a heavenly blue stream "woraus der Goldsand hin und wieder blinkt" (I, 132, 17), and when they end, Hyperion exclaims "nun sind wir wieder sterblich, Diotima!" (I, 133, 4 f.). Other exclamations too observe the pervasive pentameter pattern: "Nein, bei der Götterunschuld eurer Liebe!" cries Notara (II, 16,

13 f.); and Alabanda implores Fate to accept him as a sacrifice "und laß die Liebenden in ihrer Freude!" (II, 93, 8 f.).

A pentameter sometimes appears in emphatic initial
and final position. Thus the twenty-third letter begins with
one: "Es ist umsonst; ich kann's mir nicht verbergen," and
ends with one: "Ich fodre von dem Schiksaal meine Seele"
(I, 106, 6; 107, 18 f.). So does a short later paragraph: "O
süßer Ton aus diesen Wonnelippen! . . . noch einmal tage,
liebes Augenlicht!" (II, 18, 11 ff.). A letter-ending describ-
ing the hero's hopeful offering to the Eurotas terminates in
a trochaic pentameter with the favorite Adonic: "Bald
umblüht das alte Leben dich wieder" (II, 42, 6 f.). The corresponding motif in the minor mode, after the catastrophe
of Misistra, produces even more pentameters:

> Ein Tag hat alle Jugend mir genommen;
> am Eurotas hat mein Leben sich müde geweint, [ach!
> am Eurotas, der in rettungsloser Schmach
> an Lacedämons Schutt vorüberklagt. . . .
> Da, da hat mich das Schiksaal abgeerndtet.
>
> (II, 49, 5–8)

Such density of metrical units seems to mark especially
the later letters. In the fifty-sixth we find, in one paragraph
of only five lines, the series

> Du bist mir nachgefolgt in meine Nacht, [nun komm!
> und laß mich dir zu deinem Lichte folgen,
> zu deiner Anmuth laß uns wiederkehren, [schönes Herz!
> o deine Ruhe laß mich wiedersehen. . .!
>
> (II, 74, 4–7)

Farther on in this same letter more pentameters strike
our ear:

in seinem Spiegel unsre Welt betrachten
                    (II, 76, 8)
wenn sie im Thau die zarten Arme baden
                    (II, 76, 13)
und hier nur rinnt der Wehmuth stiller Thau
                    (II, 78, 11)
Sollt' ich nun hingehn und auch diß begraben?
                    (II, 79, 1f.)

In Diotima's last letter we find this unbroken passage:

er war mir ja willkommen, dieser Gram,
er gab dem Tode, den ich in mir trug,
Gestalt und Anmuth; deinem Lieblinge
zur Ehre stirbst du, konnt' ich nun mir sagen.
                    (II, 99, 5–7)

In the prolonged accusation of the next-to-last letter, which has in general a prosaic movement, there is nevertheless a sprinkling of verse units:

Es ist ein hartes Wort und dennoch sag' ichs
                    (II, 112, 18)
Handwerker siehst du, aber keine Menschen
                    (II, 113, 1)
Ein jeder treibt das Seine, wirst du sagen, . . .
Nur muß er es mit ganzer Seele treiben
                    (II, 113, 7 f.)
und Unschuld zaubert in ein schuldig Herz,
wenn von der Sonne warmem Strale berauscht,
der Sclave seine Ketten froh vergißt
                    (II, 115, 2–4)
so bleibt der Deutsche doch in seinem Fach'
                    (II, 115, 7)

der Erde Quellen und der Morgenthau
erfrischen euern Hain; könnt ihr auch das?
(II, 115, 16 f.)
Ihr sorgt und sinnt, dem Schiksaal zu entlaufen
(II, 116, 1 f.)
Es ist auf Erden alles unvollkommen
(II, 117, 6)
und gerne mag der Fremde sich verweilen
(II, 118, 5 f.)
der Knechtsinn wächst, mit ihm der grobe Muth
(II, 118, 9 f.)
zum Fluche wird der Seegen jedes Jahrs
(II, 118, 12)

Again we find a pentameter followed by a hexameter:

da ist des Lebens beste Lust hinweg,
und jeder andre Stern ist besser, denn die Erde
(II, 118, 7 f.).

In one evocative, melodious passage near the end of the
story, "wenn ich hinauf, wo wild die Rose um den Steinpfad wuchs, den warmen Hügel gieng" (II, 119, 18 f.), we
have one pentameter (between the commas) enclosed in
another. This last, high-pitched letter, as one might expect,
contains from beginning to end a good many imbedded
verses (counting again only complete sense units):

Ich wollte nun aus Deutschland wieder fort
(II, 119, 2)
wie konnt' ich noch an andre Dinge denken
(II, 119, 7 f.)
Und so geschah mir überall, du Lieber!
(II, 119, 16 f.)

[109]

und alle die Inseln, die er zärtlich hegt
(11, 120, 1 f.)
o wie der Mond, der noch am Himmel blieb,
die Lust des Tags zu theilen, so stand ich
(II, 120, 11 f.)
wo rings die dunkeln Eichhöhn mich umrauschten
(II, 120, 17)
O Sonne, o ihr Lüfte, rief ich dann
(II, 121, 6)
hätt' ich so gern doch weniger gewußt
(II, 121, 10)
Einst saß ich fern im Feld', an einem Brunnen
(II, 121, 18)
Es war der schönste Mittag, den ich kenne
(II, 121, 19 f.)
allein war meine Liebe mit dem Frühling
(II, 122, 4 f.)
so kehren sie zu deiner Wurzel wieder
(II, 123, 8)
und einiges, ewiges, glühendes Leben ist alles
(II, 124, 9 f.).

The last example is an unusual combination of anacrusis, dactyls, and a trochee; the final pronouncement of the book ends characteristically in an Adonic.

Other metrical patterns occur, though less prominently than hexameters and pentameters. We note a pair of trochaic tetrameters: "meine Liebe war begraben/mit der Todten, die ich liebte" (I, 106, 18 f.—The passage could also be read as four x x ' x feet). Or a tetrameter and pentameter may be joined: "Zu wem so laut das Schiksaal spricht,/der darf auch lauter sprechen mit dem Schiksaal" (II, 70, 7 f.). One iambic-paced sentence consists of two pentameters separated by a tetrameter:

[110]

Wer solch ein Schiksaal zu ergründen denkt,
der flucht am Ende sich und allem,
und doch hat keine Seele Schuld daran.

(II, 99, 1–3)

The horrified Alpine image for suddenly lost happiness
ends with two uniform dactylic-trochaic tetrameters that
anticipate the falling/abyss motif of the *Schiksaalslied*:

über die schnéidenden Záken hináb,
dích in die dämmernde Tíefe zu stürzen

(I, 51, 2 f.)

A sentence in the description of the crossing to Kalaurea
reads like an iambic-anapaestic trimeter:

Man ließ im schwebenden Schiffe
die Erde hinter sich liegen,
wie eine köstliche Speise,
wenn der heilige Wein gereicht wird.

(I, 86, 8–10).

Alabanda, aglow with the feeling of rejuvenation, apos-
trophizes *Jugend* in a lilting dactylic measure: "dann will
ich trinken aus deinem Quell, / dann will ich leben und
lieben" (II, 29, 16 f.), and this tetrameter-trimeter movement can be felt to the end of the letter, which closes with
the Adonic finial that might well be called Hölderlin's
hallmark.

XI. *Schiksaalslied*

In only one place is the pervading lyricism of this novel
apparent to the eye as well as the ear, namely in the well-
known *Schiksaalslied* (II, 94 f.), which marks the lowest
ebb in the hero's fortunes, after he has lost his friend
and (as he does not yet know) his beloved Diotima.
Even the passerby can see that this is "poetry"; yet it is no
more "poetic" than other passages in *Hyperion*. Had Hölderlin chosen to run it into his prose text, say after a
"dacht' ich," instead of designating it as a song sung to a
lute and setting it off in staggered lines and stanzas, how
many readers, one wonders, would have recognized it and
isolated it as a poem? The line between Hölderlin's poetic
prose and the prose-poetic (logœdic) verse of this piece
is very thin.[1]

---

[1] For the classification of the meter of the *Schiksaalslied* as logœdic,
and the theory of "Freie Rhythmen" as an imitation of the Greek logœdic
measures, see the remarks of Steven T. Byington in *Goethe's Poems,* ed.
Martin Schütze (Boston [Ginn], 1916), pp. 269 ff.

On first view, the poem may seem utterly simple. One notes at once the timeless, "classical" simplicity of its language and imagery, its restraint even in the utterance of anguish; and on the other hand its "romantic" sense of tragic transiency and undertone of *Sehnsucht*. Some of Hölderlin's favorite adjectives: "heilig," "seelig," "ewig," "still," are here.[2] One can describe the metrical structure of two-, three-, and four-stress lines, observing the predominance of dipodic verses and the frequency of adonic and (rarer) choriambic ones. One can write out a scheme of the consonant and especially the sonorous vowel sounds, like bell notes, high, middle, and low. But it proves impossible to pattern or structure or "explain" the exquisite grace and music of this composition.

Though the theme is an antithesis, the contrast is not carried through in calculated detail, as in many a lesser "Gegensatzgedicht." The gods see clearly, while men are blind; but there is no darkness opposed to the gods' light, no hard footing to balance their fleecy floor. Rather, the essential antinomy is one between assured permanence and unpredictable change. On the side of the divinities, eternal youth of spirit, symbolized by the chaste bud that never opens and hence never fades, that is immune to time and vicissitude. The gods are here represented as exempt from fate—not the profoundest view, either with the Greeks or with Hölderlin—and they are thought of as "above" in a conventional heaven like the personalized gods of the mythology books, not indwelling as Nature's great divinities. They are gently bathed in luminous heavenly airs. With level, quiet gaze their blissful eyes see clearly to in-

[2] These are among Klopstock's favorite adjectives too. The deep kinship between these two poets is indicated very briefly in my article "On Rereading Klopstock," *PMLA*, LXVII (1952), pp. 751 f.

finity. If the poem's movement were to be graphed, the gods' line would be a horizontal without end, Man's a jagged "staircase" downward, equally endless for the race.

The poem shows Hölderlin's characteristic tripartite structure; it consists of three stanzas with line numbers divisible by three: respectively six, nine, and nine verses. Moreover, each stanza can be roughly divided into three parts: stanza one—addressed to the gods—consists of two sentences and one clause, each of two lines; stanza two—said of the gods—is likewise tripartite (lines 7–8, 9–12, 13–15); in stanza three—said of Man—the division is less obvious, but again we can distinguish two sentences (16 f. and 18 ff.) and one clause, though in this case the second sentence is completed after the clause. In the first two stanzas there is no action, or only the gentlest, while stanza three is marked by violent action. The very syntax and punctuation accord with the progress of the thought: the god stanzas are contained units, suspended, held in balance, whereas the mankind stanza, unstopped, rushes inexorably downward to the final "hinab" which signifies a direction, not an ending.

The *Götter/Menschen* antithesis which is here merely stated, not resolved, the pathetic contrast of the lot of mortals and of gods, was a commonplace of that age. We find it in Goethe's "Grenzen der Menschheit" and "Das Göttliche," in the "Parzenlied" of *Iphigenie*,[3] in Schiller's "Das Ideal und das Leben." In thought, Hölderlin adds nothing to the *topos;* his contribution consists in lucid vision and expressive form. The theology of the poem

---

[3] This, like the *Schiksaalslied*, was not "made" by the hero(ine) for the present occasion, but is the quoted utterance of another person (Amme/ Adamas) during the speaker's early years. Not comprehended then, it is now recalled as tragically appropriate.

represents an immature stage for Hölderlin and his hero. Both will come to see the relation of men and gods in deeper terms. Both will accept the bent or bowed line, not the horizontal, as the condition and emblem of Man's achievement and glory as well as his tragedy.[4] In this very letter, Diotima's valedictory wisdom gives the answer to the conventional dichotomy: "Vollendung" is attainable in "Wechsel" as well as in "Beständigkeit" (II, 103). This in turn leads Hyperion to the momentary insight—again in this same rich letter (II, 106 f.)—which, as Lawrence Ryan has well said, negates the present negation.[5] The insight is one that "festgehalten, überglänzte jeden Schatz," but Hyperion, as we have seen, is not yet able to hold it fast.

It seems to me that the difference between such a manifest poem and other passages at crucial points in the story is chiefly one of degree of lyrical concentration and structuring. For example, the sublime antiphonal hymn in which the lovers avow their spiritual bond with Nature and plight their troth as it were on her altar (II, 17; thirty-sixth letter) could be arranged in three strophes (corresponding to Hölderlin's three paragraphs) in some such manner as this:

Längst, o Natur! ist unser Leben
Eines mit dir,
und himmlischjugendlich,
wie du und deine Götter all',
ist unsre eigne Welt durch Liebe.

---

[4] E.g., I, 71, 3 ff., and poems like *Lebenslauf*. In reality, of course, the arrow's flight, except at close range, describes an arc, not a straight line; and return to the point of origin ("woher ich kam") calls for a *Kreis*, not a *Bogen*. Hölderlin's imagery is lyrical, not logical, in origin.

[5] L. Ryan, *Hölderlins "Hyperion"* (1965), p. 209.

In deinen Hainen wandelten wir,
und waren, wie du,
an deinen Quellen saßen wir,
und waren, wie du,
dort über die Berge giengen wir,
mit deinen Kindern, den Sternen,
wie du.

Da wir uns ferne waren,
da, wie Harfengelispel,
unser kommend Entzüken uns erst tönte,
da wir uns fanden,
da kein Schlaf mehr war
und alle Töne in uns erwachten
zu des Lebens vollen Akkorden,
göttliche Natur!
da waren wir immer, wie du,
und nun auch da wir scheiden
und die Freude stirbt,
sind wir, wie du,
voll Leidens und doch gut,
drum soll ein reiner Mund uns zeugen,
daß unsre Liebe heilig ist und ewig,
so wie du.

The stately rhythms, the invocations and refrains, the melodious language and musical imagery, the high pitch of controlled emotion authenticate this as a virtual lyric of Hölderlinian type. This is not to claim that we have discovered a second *Schiksaalslied* to rival the first—who would even presume to measure the distance between them? It is merely to suggest the quality of the deep lyric matrix of *Hyperion* from which the one gem was fully cut.

In the present "poem" too the mood is solemn and sad; there is a strong implication of finality and death; the past tenses, especially in Diotima's lines ("stanza" two), seem to sum up a life and love soon to be ended and taken up into Nature's "All." Thus Hyperion, in his next letter to Diotima, can speak of the "death" of this parting and of their love as now removed from time and fate (II, 21, 14; 22, 10–12). And yet there is a positive "existential" value in the lovers' hymn; it is a beautiful and courageous assertion of Hölderlin's blended ideals of Nature and Love; and one may feel in it, though the feeling is not required for its artistic appreciation, the heartbeat of the poet's personal life.

The *Schiksaalslied* and, in their degree, the emergent lyrics of other passages in this novel sound like a preluding of the great poetry in rhymeless free-rhythmic form that was yet to come. Hölderlin was not in principle opposed to rhyme, as Klopstock was, but rhymed verse, such as he wrote in his youth in the train of Schiller, was never germane to him, and it is significant that he reverted to it after his mind was gone. With *Hyperion*, however, he established himself in the broad zone of unrhymed but measured, rhythmical, and musical prose-poetic utterance that suited his artistic individuality and "wave-length." Hence we may credit *Hyperion* with a pivotal importance in Hölderlin's career.

XII. *Poetry in Prose*

The chief literary distinction of *Hyperion* is its prose-poetic style. The analysis of it, in its unconscious ways and conscious means, presents a seemingly inexhaustible subject for study. To exhibit Hölderlin's stylistic art fully, one would need virtually to excerpt his novel under such rubrics as alliteration and assonance, antithesis and balance, figurative language, symbolism, and others. On the following pages, only a few representative examples of such features will be discussed, as a supplement to our previous observations.

The feature most obvious to even a casual reader is the use of comparison. Hölderlin's text is studded with the *wie* of almost incessant similes which, bringing in often distant correlates, greatly extend the imaginative range of his writing. Most typically, they open up the background of Nature, near and remote, as when the despondent hero likens himself to a fallen fir that lies by a brook, hiding its withered crown in the water (I, 29), or when the night sky

[118]

is seen metaphorically as a dark meadow filled with the shining flowers of other worlds (II, 76). Sometimes, in keeping with Hölderlin's basic three-rhythm, there is a triad of similes: "Wie das Saitenspiel der himmlischen Muse über den uneinigen Elementen, herrschten Diotima's stille Gedanken über den Trümmern. Wie der Mond aus zartem Gewölke, hob sich ihr Geist aus schönem Leiden empor; das himmlische Mädchen stand in seiner Wehmuth da, wie die Blume, die in der Nacht am lieblichsten duftet" (I, 154). Here we have a blend of the mythic-musical and the Klopstockian with a Romantic nocturne, and again the cadences rest on adonics and choriambs.

Hölderlin's similes often represent an ebullience of lyric emotion. For instance, the series of quickly shifting pictures that express Hyperion's disillusionment with Alabanda and his associations (I, 60, 6–18) go far beyond the function of explication; they embellish the fact with passionate invention. Like many passages in the *Messias*, they illuminate not so much the event as its inward effect, its "Seelenwirkung."

Metaphors are less frequent in *Hyperion* than similes, possibly because the metaphor is by nature more direct and dramatic, while the simile offers more scope for lyrical-emotional elaboration; but the distinction is not sharp. Typical in its Biblical cadence and imagery and its chiastic order is the lover's declaration "eine Sonne ist der Mensch, allsehend, allverklärend, wenn er liebt, und liebt er nicht, so ist er eine dunkle Wohnung, wo ein rauchend Lämpchen brennt" (I, 133).

To the Bible which he knew so well Hölderlin also owes a liking for parallel construction: "die Helden haben ihren Ruhm, die Weisen ihre Lehrlinge verloren. Große Thaten, wenn sie nicht ein edel Volk vernimmt, sind mehr

[119]

nicht als ein gewaltiger Schlag vor eine dumpfe Stirne, und hohe Worte, wenn sie nicht in hohen Herzen wiedertönen, sind, wie ein sterbend Blatt, das in den Koth herunterrauscht" (I, 47). Again, with characteristic musical reference: "Weint nicht, wenn das Treflichste verblüht! bald wird es sich verjüngen! Trauert nicht, wenn eures Herzens Melodie verstummt! bald findet eine Hand sich wieder, es zu stimmen!" (I, 92). This feature too is sometimes tripled: "Wem einmal, so, wie dir, die ganze Seele belaidiget war, der ruht nicht mehr in einzelner Freude, wer so, wie du, das fade Nichts gefühlt, erheitert in höchstem Geiste sich nur, wer so den Tod erfuhr, wie du, erholt allein sich unter den Göttern" (II, 68).[1]

Rhythm and sound, cadence and melody, are a major part of the magic of Hölderlin's style, but one can generalize about them only up to a certain point. It is evident that he (a musician) not only had a fine musical ear which unconsciously guided his writing, but also that he worked consciously to produce euphonious wording, a pleasing as well as expressive rhythmical sequence, a sustained melodic line, and to avoid harshness and hiatus. The choice of words, the distribution of emphasis in stressed and unstressed syllables; expansions and contractions such as the insertion or elision of an unaccented e[2] or the filling-in with inconspicuous particles like *es* or *so*; departures from customary syntax and word order; the arrangement of an-

---

[1] Italicized (the only passage so printed) in the original. Just before this, a triple parallel occurs in question form: II, 68, 4–7. Both passages end with adonics. Parallelism in the Biblical manner, sometimes tripled, is also a feature of *Werther*, e.g. the third paragraph of "am 20. Januar."

[2] For example, in II, 10, 10: "Du sollst gehn, sollst gehen, stolzer Mensch!", the rhythm would have been spoiled had Hölderlin not varied "gehn" to "gehen" in the second instance. In "Ich seh', ich sehe wie das enden muß" (I, 136), eliding the *e* of "sehe" would undo a pentameter.

swering consonants and vowels—all these contribute to the music of this lyrical prose.[3]

A good example is the magnificent paragraph in an early letter (the sixth) in which Hölderlin evokes his dream of a Greek landscape—it is identified as that around Smyrna as seen by the young Hyperion on his lone *Wanderschaft*:

> Zur Linken stürzt' und jauchzte, wie ein Riese, der Strom in die Wälder hinab, vom Marmorfelsen, der über mir hieng, wo der Adler spielte mit seinen Jungen, wo die Schneegipfel hinauf in den blauen Aether glänzten; rechts wälzten Wetterwolken sich her über den Wäldern des Sipylus; ich fühlte nicht den Sturm, der sie trug, ich fühlte nur ein Lüftchen in den Loken, aber ihren Donner hört' ich, wie man die Stimme der Zukunft hört, und ihre Flammen sah ich, wie das ferne Licht der geahneten Gottheit. Ich wandte mich südwärts und gieng weiter. Da lag es offen vor mir, das ganze paradiesische Land, das der Cayster durchströmt, durch so manchen reizenden Umweg, als könnt' er nicht lange genug verweilen in all' dem Reichtum und der Lieblichkeit, die ihn umgiebt. Wie die Zephyre, irrte mein Geist von Schönheit zu Schönheit seelig umher, vom fremden friedlichen Dörfchen, das tief unten am Berge lag, bis hinein, wo die Gebirgkette des Messogis dämmert.

(I, 33/34)

---

[3] It is instructive to compare the close of the sixteenth letter: "Was ist alles, was in Jahrtausenden die Menschen thaten und dachten, gegen Einen Augenblick der Liebe?" (I, 98, 12 f.), with the inaccurate reproduction in H. H. Borcherdt, *Der Roman der Goethezeit*, [1949], p. 345: "Was ist gegenüber einem Augenblick der Liebe alles, was in Jahrtausenden die Menschen taten und dachten!" The sense is rendered, but the rhythm and emphasis, the tone (! vs. ?), the rise and fall of the sentence are destroyed by the seemingly slight rearrangement.

The paragraph is divided into two almost equal parts by the pivotal sentence "Ich wandte mich südwärts." In both parts, but especially in the first, we note some of Hölderlin's favorite motifs and symbols: the mountain torrent rushing downward, rocky crags, snowy peaks gleaming against the blue aether, the eagle and its brood, clouds rolling up over forests, thunder as the voice of the future, and lightning which to Hölderlin was the supreme manifestation of the numinous.[4] Then, with Hölderlinian balance and antithesis, a quieter music in the second part: a lovely, fruitful valley with a lingering river that seems loth to leave it, villages nestling on the lower slopes, and the whole picture terminated by a mountain range dim in the distance. The first part is heroic, the second idyllic: the storm becomes a zephyr, and the rivers are humanized in opposite characters.

The colors in this picture are not emphasized, yet are perceptible: the blue of the sky, the white of the summits, the dark gray of the thunderclouds, the various greens of forest and field, the misty blue of mountains on the horizon—all are part of the "himmlisch unendlich Farbenspiel" of the spring (II, 33, 8 f.). But more expressive are the rhythmical phrasing and the sounds: the musical repetitions, the alliterations on w, l, and other consonants, the sonorous answering vowels, the rich, placid a's that introduce the fertile valley: "Da lag es offen vor mir, das ganze paradiesische Land."

Apostrophe, invocation, question, exclamation abound

---

[4] "Denn unter allem, was ich schauen kann von Gott, ist dieses Zeichen mir das auserkorene geworden" (letter of December 4, 1801, to Böhlendorff; StA 6, No. 236, 11. 72 f.). It might be added that "Zukunft" in the text just before has, as elsewhere in Hölderlin, some of its etymological force of a "drawing near" (of the divine).

in the text of *Hyperion*. The question mark, the "O," the
exclamation point are frequent. The very punctuation indicates the lyrical excitement of this style. A brief example
is the close of the twenty-seventh letter: "O ihr Uferweiden
des Lethe!/ihr abendröthlichen Pfade in Elysiums Wäl-
dern!/ihr Lilien an den Bächen des Thals!/ihr Rosen-
kränze des Hügels!//Ich glaub' an euch, in dieser freundlichen Stunde,/und spreche zu meinem Herzen:/dort
findest du sie wieder,/und alle Freude, die du verlorst" (I,
122).[5] Again we can observe symmetrical balance in two
sentences of approximately equal length, the one exclama-
tory, the other declarative; the first fervidly invoking four
symbolic mythical scenes in a future that is tinged with the
past; the other with equal fervor avowing its faith in a
reunion there. One could arrange the passage in eight
rhythmical prose-poetic lines, as indicated by the virgules.

The second letter is an example of Hölderlin's use of
parallel and contrasting sentence rhythms. It opens with
somber cadences in short sentences that fall heavily with a
Biblical or Ossianic ring:

> Ich habe nichts, wovon ich sagen möchte [= könnte], es
> sey mein eigen.
> Fern und todt sind meine Geliebten, und ich vernehme
> durch keine Stimme von ihnen nichts mehr.
> Mein Geschäft auf Erden ist aus. . . .
> Ruhmlos und einsam kehr' ich zurük.[6]

(I, 9)

---

[5] The imagery and thought are related to those of *Der Abschied* (2.
Fassung), especially the ending. There are many such links between Hölderlin's novel and his poems.

[6] This sentence, consisting of an adonic and a choriamb, shows how
closely related these two favorite final cadences are. They again appear
together in the last quotation of our paragraph: "–mént dĕs Bĕsínnĕns
wírft mĭch hĕráb."

[123]

Then by contrast the longer wave-lengths and "rising" rhythms of a grateful hymn to Nature, beginning with a triple "noch" (one of Hölderlin's most significant adverbs): "Aber du scheinst noch, Sonne des Himmels! Du grünst noch, heilige Erde! Noch rauschen die Ströme ins Meer, und schattige Bäume säuseln im Mittag," and so on into a rapturous love song and confession of faith, the triple anaphora "Eines zu sein mit Allem, . . . Eines zu seyn mit Allem, was lebt, . . . Eines zu seyn mit Allem, was lebt!" being developed in three enlarging paragraphs. Then this vision vanishes in doubt and dejection, and the short, falling cadences return: "Auf dieser Höhe steh' ich oft, . . . Aber ein Moment des Besinnens wirft mich herab," and thus to the end of the letter (I, 10–12).

Sometimes Hölderlin mingles short and long measures, for instance in the last paragraph of the twelfth letter, to express both eagerness and contemplation. It begins with a short sentence in chiastic order: "[1] Der Boden ist grüner geworden, offner das Feld." Then follow two longer double sentences which in their movement balance each other, each composed of two- and three-stress units as marked by our virgules: "[2] Unendlich steht,/mit der freudigen Kornblume gemischt,/der goldene Waizen da,/ und licht und heiter/steigen tausend hoffnungsvolle Gipfel/aus der Tiefe des Hains./[3] Zart und groß/durchirret den Raum/jede Linie der Fernen;/wie Stuffen gehn die Berge bis zur Sonne unaufhörlich hinter einander hinauf." (The first part of this third sentence has a hexameter character; the latter part, with its pauseless movement upward, is a sort of inversion of the last lines of the *Schiksaalslied*.) Then comes a short three-stress unit: "[4] Der ganze Himmel ist rein"; then another balanced double sentence, suggesting Klopstock and Hölty in its delicacy of perception, which is made up of triadic units but reads like a continuum: "[5] Das weiße Licht ist nur/über den Aether gehaucht,/und, wie ein silbern Wölkchen,/wallt der schüchterne Mond/am hellen Tage vorüber" (I, 84). Here too, colors, though not obtrusive, are present: the blue of the cornflower, the gold of the wheat, the white haze diffused over the blue sky, the silver of the daytime moon. The "pathetic fallacy" is in evidence, as is Hölderlin's extraordinary sense for the rhythm in landscape lines, the movement of the hills, which is a feature in several poems.[7]

Like a short musical prelude, the opening of the twenty-sixth letter, with its falling accents, sets a mood of elegiac sadness: "Ich baue meinem Hérzĕn eĭn Gráb, damit es ruhen möge; ich spínnĕ mĭch eín, weil überall es Winter ist; in seeligen Erinnerungen hüll' ich vor dem Stúrmĕ mĭch eín" (I, 110). Again the Hölderlinian triadism: three variations on the theme of protective withdrawal, three related but different metaphors, three sentence units of almost equal length and similar syntax. At three places ("Herzen ein Grab," "spinne mich ein," and "Sturme mich ein") choriambs add terminal weight.

Doubles and triads, and the verbal music produced by repetition and climactic variation, are illustrated by Diotima's avowal of her love: "abtrünnig bin ich geworden von Mai und Sommer und Herbst, und achte des Tages und der Nacht nicht, wie sonst, gehöre dem Himmel und der Erde nicht mehr, gehöre nur Einem, Einem, aber die

---

[7] E.g., *Der Wanderer* (1. Fassung): "Fernhin schlich das haagre Gebirg"; *Rükkehr in die Heimath:* "Ihr woogenden Gebirg!"; *Stutgard:* "so ziehn die / Berge voran"; *Der Mutter Erde:* "Gebirg, / Das hochaufwoogend von Meer zu Meer / Hinziehet über die Erde"; *Der Rhein:* "fliehn / . . . zusammensinkend die Berge." *Heidelberg* is a striking example of pervasive movement in a landscape; see my interpretation of this ode in *GR* 37 (1962), especially pp. 158 f.

Blüthe des Mai's und die Flamme des Sommers und die
Reife des Herbsts, die Klarheit des Tags und der Ernst der
Nacht, und Erd' und Himmel ist mir in diesem Einen
vereint!" (I, 135). Here again we have a diction on the
borderline between prose and a free form of verse.

Some of the most beautiful lyrical rhythms of Hölderlin's prose are to be found in the concluding letter. From
all its wealth one specimen might be chosen, two related
paragraphs near the beginning:

> Und wenn ich oft des Morgens, wie die Kranken zum
> Heilquell, auf den Gipfel des Gebirgs stieg, durch die
> schlafenden Blumen, aber vom süßen Schlummer gesät-
> tiget, neben mir die lieben Vögel aus dem Busche flogen,
> im Zwielicht taumelnd und begierig nach dem Tag, und
> die regere Luft nun schon die Gebete der Thäler, die Stim-
> men der Heerde und die Töne der Morgengloken herauf-
> trug, und jezt das hohe Licht, das göttlichheitre den ge-
> wohnten Pfad daherkam, die Erde bezaubernd mit unsterb-
> lichem Leben, daß ihr Herz erwarmt' und all' ihre Kinder
> wieder sich fühlten—o wie der Mond, der noch am Himmel
> blieb, die Lust des Tags zu theilen, so stand ich Einsamer
> dann auch über den Ebnen und weinte Liebesthränen zu
> den Ufern hinab und den glänzenden Gewässern und
> konnte lange das Auge nicht wenden.
>
> Oder des Abends, wenn ich fern ins Thal hinein gerieth,
> zur Wiege des Quells, wo rings die dunkeln Eichhöhn mich
> umrauschten, mich, wie einen Heiligsterbenden, in ihren
> Frieden die Natur begrub, wenn nun die Erd' ein Schatte
> war, und unsichtbares Leben durch die Zweige säuselte,
> durch die Gipfel, und über den Gipfeln still die Abend-
> wolke stand, ein glänzend Gebirg, wovon herab zu mir des
> Himmels Stralen, wie die Wasserbäche flossen, um den
> durstigen Wanderer zu tränken—(II, 120, 3–121, 5)

These twin paragraphs illustrate Hölderlin's liking for balanced or antiphonal composition: the first is a morning, the second an evening song. The first has in general an upward, aspiring, more energetic movement, with verbs of action prominent, and many high notes in its rich music of alliterating consonants and vowels. It rises in a prolonged subordinate clause ("wenn . . .") to a climax in the sunrise ("das hohe Licht"), pivots in the eleventh line on a dash, and descends rapidly in a much shorter main clause which parallels the hero and the humanized moon and brings the emotional release in tears of love and gratitude.

The pendant to this is the second paragraph with its "darker," slower sounds and rhythms, its opening of the soul inward instead of outward. It is similarly constructed, with a long "buildup" of subordinate clauses rising again to a light-climax (the rays of the sun*set*) and again a short descent that brings relief to the parched wayfarer. The summary and resolution to both paragraphs is in the brief "coda" which follows: "O Sonne, o ihr Lüfte, rief ich dann, bei euch allein noch lebt mein Herz, wie unter Brüdern!" (II, 121, 6 f.). Here, as in the other two parts, verse units and favorite cadences are again discernible.[8] It is not a great step from such passages to poem pairs like the odes *Abendphantasie* and *Des Morgens* (StA 1, 301 f.); they show a similar conception of Man before Nature and a similar Hölderlinian structure of rise, fall, and resolution.

The last letter constitutes a conclusion insofar as it weaves together into a final symphony all of Hölderlin's principal motifs: the eternal beauties of earth and sky, Aether and Light, Sun and Moon, Nature with its im-

[8] The "coda" itself is another example of a pentameter/hexameter sequence.

mortal gods, and features of the beloved native landscape. The great ideas of *Liebe* and *Schönheit, Wechsel* and *Wiederkehr, Begeisterung, Leiden* and *Freude,* are invoked once more. The great words shine forth from their setting in the text: "Flamme," "Freiheit," "Frieden," "ewige Jugend," "blühende Bäume," "klare Bäche," "lebendige Töne," "O du mit deinen Göttern, Natur!" "Ihr Quellen der Erd'! ihr Blumen! und ihr Wälder und ihr Adler und du brüderliches Licht!" "O Seele! Seele! Schönheit der Welt!" And, life's crowning glory and loveliest flower, Diotima as a continuing spiritual presence.

One cannot resist the feeling that Hölderlin, forgetting or transcending in a surge of lyric emotion the doubts he had planted in earlier letters and his final ambiguity "Nächstens mehr," meant this to be the full climax and conclusion of his novel. At the opening of the final *Buch,* Hyperion had told Bellarmin that he would now conduct him down into the deepest depths of his sorrow and then upward again "zur Stelle, wo ein neuer Tag uns anglänzt" (II, 59)—a motif like that of the opening of the *Purgatorio,* where Dante and his guide emerge from the terrors and dark of Hell into the clear morning light.[9] This forecast indicates that Hölderlin conceived his ending (in the final letter) as positive, as the dawn of a new day, the start of a new life epoch—perhaps with its own story to be told: this might be the deeper meaning of "Nächstens mehr."

If the burden of the bitter penultimate letter was the loss of Nature, the theme of the last is the recovery and glorification of Nature as the realm of divine beauty and the place of ultimate healing, as the great Life in which individual existences with their bliss and agony are gath-

[9] See C. H. Herford, *Goethe* (London, 1913), p. 73, where the parallel is applied to the opening of the second part of *Faust.*

ered up forever. According to this reading, Hyperion yields himself up finally to "der seeligen Natur" and its benign powers. The return to Nature in a religious spirit would seem to be Hölderlin's solution both for his hero and for mankind. This creed, preached with all the fervor and the lyrical splendor of which his prose was capable, makes the close of *Hyperion* in truth its last word. As the outcome of a cogent novel plot, the reasoning mind, we have seen, finds it variously questionable; as the finale of a superb prose elegy on love and loss and spiritual rebirth, it carries us along to a consummation that our hearts do not question.

Bibliography

Bibliography

The following bibliography, added at the editors' and publisher's suggestion, is only a small selection from the voluminous literature on Hölderlin (which can be expected to swell in the coming bicentenary year). It includes some of the works cited in my text, plus a few others that I have found valuable; together they might be considered a first and basic Hölderlin bibliography.

The scholarly edition, establishing the standard text and superseding all earlier editions, is the "Grosse Stuttgarter Ausgabe" (StA): *Hölderlin. Sämtliche Werke, . . .* herausgegeben von Friedrich Beissner (Stuttgart, 1943 ff.; of eight volumes, 1–7, part 1, have appeared thus far). *Hyperion* is in volume 3, edited by Beissner; letters by and to Hölderlin, and other documents, are in volumes 6 and 7, edited by Adolf Beck. The "Kleine Stuttgarter Ausgabe," edited by Beissner, in smaller format (1944 ff.), contains the same texts as the large StA, but with much less apparatus. There is also a thin-paper, one-volume edition by Beissner (Frankfurt [Insel], 1961).

The chief repository for Hölderlin research is in the publications of the Hölderlin-Gesellschaft in Tübingen:

(a) *Hölderlin-Jahrbuch* (which began as *Iduna,* 1944, one number only), 1948 ff., containing current bibliographies; (b) *Schriften der Hölderlin-Gesellschaft,* (1949 ff.).

An indispensable handbook for biographical and bibliographical information is Lawrence Ryan's *Friedrich Hölderlin* in the Sammlung Metzler (2nd ed., Stuttgart, 1967).

Wilhelm Michel's *Das Leben Friedrich Hölderlins,* 3. Aufl. (Bremen, 1949), available in reprints by the Wissenschaftliche Buchgesellschaft (Darmstadt, 1963), and the Insel-Verlag (Frankfurt, 1967) is the best life-and-works account. Ronald Peacock's *Hölderlin* (London, 1938), not a biography but an interpretation and appreciation, is the best book in English.

Wilhelm Dilthey's pioneer essay "Hölderlin" (originally 1867), incorporated in his *Das Erlebnis und die Dichtung* (1906 and later prints) still has value. Other monographs and studies of importance are:

Friedrich Beissner, *Hölderlin.* Reden und Aufsätze (Weimar, 1961)

Paul Böckmann, *Hölderlin und seine Götter* (München, 1935); second edition in preparation.

Wilhelm Böhm, *Hölderlin,* 2 vols. (Halle a. S., 1928, 1930)

Romano Guardini, *Hölderlin.* Weltbild und Frömmigkeit, 2. Aufl. (München, 1955)

Johannes Hoffmeister, *Hölderlin und die Philosophie,* 2. Aufl. (Leipzig, 1944)

Hölderlin. Gedenkschrift . . . , herausgegeben von Paul Kluckhohn (Tübingen, 1943), 2 Aufl. 1944

Ernst Müller, *Hölderlin*. Studien zur Geschichte
  seines Geistes (Stuttgart, 1944)
Hans-Heinrich Schottmann, *Metapher und Vergleich
  in der Sprache Friedrich Hölderlins* (Bonn, 1959)
Karl Viëtor, *Die Lyrik Hölderlins* (Frankfurt a.M.,
  1921)
Viëtor's edition of *Die Briefe der Diotima* (1921 and
  many later issues) has recently been superseded by
  Adolf Beck's definitive edition in StA 7, 1, pp. 58–
  124.
On *Hyperion,* the most important previous monograph
is Lawrence Ryan's *Hölderlins "Hyperion."* Exzentrische
Bahn und Dichterberuf (Stuttgart, 1965).

Index

A. PERSONS

INDEX